The premise of *Designed to Lead* engages an important and necessary topic for the local church today. The local church must be a place where God's people are equipped to lead wherever God has placed them. Eric and Kevin have passion, experience, and knowledge in this area that will greatly help God's church.

—**Matt Chandler**, Lead Pastor of Teaching,
The Village Church, Flower Mound, Texas

The cries are loud and clear: "We need more leaders in our church!" Now, at last, you have a biblical and practical pathway to increase the leaders in your church. I am so thankful for the two great leaders who wrote this book, Eric Geiger and Kevin Peck. I am also excited about the impact this book will have on countless churches in the world for the glory of God!

—**Dr. Thom S. Rainer**, President and CEO,
LifeWay Christian Resources

In a world obsessed with numbers, Kevin and Eric are refreshing voices fighting for Christ-centered depth. In a culture that praises power, they remind us that lasting impact is found in humility and sacrifice, as modeled by Jesus. I've observed both of these men lead and they lead well, with honesty, intentionality, and ultimately a sincere commitment to see Christ change lives from the pulpits to the cubicles. Prepare to enjoy serving Jesus again.

—**Jennie Allen**, author of *Anything and Restless*,
Visionary Leader of IF:Gathering

Kevin Peck and Eric Geiger are transformational leaders of this generation. That's why it's no surprise that *Designed to Lead* is an invaluable call on the church to produce leaders with conviction, courage, and compassion. This book will be an asset for the church for many years to come.

—**Russell Moore**, President, Ethics and
Religious Liberty Commission

Anyone can write about leadership. But being a proven leader worth following is more of an extraordinary find. As Mark Twain said, "It's the difference between the lightning and the lightning bug." These guys have proven they can write but more importantly can lead. I love the premise of the book, the style and the usefulness. Read. Learn. Follow.

—**Dr. Stephen R. Graves**, CEO coach and author

If churches are going to help people live on mission and influence those around them, then churches must develop leaders, not just for their churches but also for the world. I am grateful for Eric and Kevin's challenge for your church to disciple and deploy leaders who represent His Kingdom to all people. *Designed to Lead* is both helpful and challenging. This will be a resource church leaders return to time and time again.

—**Ed Stetzer**, Billy Graham Distinguished Chair, Wheaton College

The church produces leaders, not just for the church but to change the world. *Designed to Lead* will assist and inspire church leaders to operate their ministries with a deep conviction to discover, equip, inspire, and send leaders out into the worlds of business, education, law, politics, medicine and ministry. This book will lead you to rethink your strategy and readjust your priorities to prepare leaders for life, leadership, and ministry in and through the local church.

—**Dr. Ronnie Floyd**, President, Southern Baptist Convention, Senior Pastor, Cross Church

It is the work of the church to identify, develop, and deploy disciples to change the world with the message of the gospel. Unfortunately, many leaders find themselves without a biblical pathway for equipping the saints to do the work of ministry. Drawing from years of experience, Eric Geiger and Kevin Peck provide a simple, reproducible process for making disciples who will in turn make disciple-makers. They have put into words what great leaders do intuitively. Take your staff through this book. You'll be glad you did!

—**Robby Gallaty**, Senior Pastor, Long Hollow Baptist Church, author of *Growing Up* and *Rediscovering Discipleship*

Peck and Geiger have done us a service in writing this. They are ambitious in their goal but winsome in their tone. I like this book. It's accessible and immensely helpful. More significantly, I will use this book. You should too.

—**Steve Timmis**, author of *Gospel-Centered Leadership*, Executive Director, Acts 29

The title *Designed to Lead* really says it all. There is not a better place to learn how to influence others than in our churches as Jesus is the ultimate Leader. Eric and Kevin do a great job communicating this truth.

—**Billy Kennedy**, head coach, men's basketball, Texas A&M

Congratulations on discovering the new gold standard for leadership development in ministry.

—**Will Mancini,** founder of Auxano, author of *God Dreams*

Designed to Lead by Kevin Peck and Eric Geiger is designed to help us all realize our God-given mandate to disciple and develop leaders. This book will help you develop the culture and the construct to reproduce leaders who will help your church accomplish the Jesus mission!

—**Dave Ferguson,** Lead Pastor, Community Christian Church, Lead Visionary, NewThing

The church must make a priority to develop new leaders who can advance the gospel into all areas of life. This book is a rich resource for understanding how to develop that culture in your church.

—**Ben Peays, PhD,** Executive Director, The Gospel Coalition

With a cogent and clear path, this monograph serves as a gold mine for identifying and equipping leaders for the marketplace and ministry. Intentionality is the missing gem in modern gospel leadership cultivation. These men have rightly placed a high view of intentionality front and center in the leadership pipeline. As a call to action, *Designed to Lead* is a mandatory read and a game-changer for all Christian leaders.

—**Dan Dumas,** author of *Live Smart*

There's a moment in every baby's life when they look in a mirror and finally recognize themselves to be a person staring back. This happens in the Christian life as well. We look into the Scriptures and see who God has created us to be and has recreated us to be in Christ. *Designed to Lead* holds the mirror steady so we can see ourselves clearly. All of us, whether we are pastors, moms, youth workers, students, and otherwise, could stand to benefit greatly from this book. Geiger and Peck have compiled a comprehensive look at our role in the mission of God, analyzed our weaknesses and blind spots, and enthusiastically communicated the power behind our leadership: the gospel. *Designed to Lead* has given me a lot to think about, and I'm very grateful.

—**Gloria Furman,** cross-cultural worker, author of *Missional Motherhood: The Everyday Ministry of Motherhood in the Grand Plan of God*

In a much needed book, *Designed to Lead* puts on paper the principles and practices that have made Kevin Peck and Eric Geiger two of the best leaders in the Church today. If you're a leader in any capacity, in or outside of the local church, this book will help take your organization to another level.

—**Dr. Matt Carter**, Pastor of Preaching,
The Austin Stone Community Church

When people ask me about who they should learn leadership from, I immediately say, "Kevin Peck." I have called him "the smartest guy I know" and many other wonderful things. But Kevin is not just a high capacity leader and visionary, he's also a humble brother who loves the gospel and Christ's church. Over the last five years, I have had the privilege of learning much from Kevin, and I'm thrilled that he and Eric Geiger (whom I also want to grow up and be like!) have put their leadership ideas in print. This book will help countless leaders and churches who desire to make disciples of all nations. I will be using it for years to come.

—**Dr. Tony Merida**, Pastor for Preaching and Vision,
Imago Dei Church, Raleigh, North Carolina

Leading and serving is built into the DNA of God's good creation. It must also be built into the DNA of God's new creation the Church. *Designed to Lead* is a superb work that will help churches do exactly that. I gladly commend this book by Peck and Geiger. It is a good gift to God's community of faith.

—**Daniel L. Akin**, President,
Southeastern Baptist Theological Seminary

Peck and Geiger model the way forward with their writing and their lives in *Designed to Lead*. They are faithful guides for facing the complex realities of leading local communities. The practical insights of this book and the "how–to's" are invaluable not as scripts to follow, but examples to emulate and build upon.

—**Daniel Montgomery**, Lead Pastor of
Sojourn Community Church, Louisville, Kentucky,
founder Sojourn Network, author,
Faithmapping, PROOF & Leadership Mosaic

DESIGNED
to
LEAD

ERIC GEIGER *and* KEVIN PECK

**THE CHURCH AND
LEADERSHIP DEVELOPMENT**

DESIGNED
to
LEAD

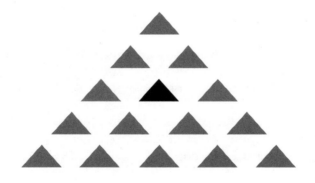

B&H
PUBLISHING GROUP

NASHVILLE, TENNESSEE

978-1-4336-9024-2

Published by B&H Publishing Group
Nashville, Tennessee

Dewey Decimal Classification: 303.3
Subject Heading: LEADERSHIP \ CHURCH \ MINISTRY

1 2 3 4 5 6 7 • 20 19 18 17 16

DEDICATION

Eric

The Geiger girls (Kaye, Eden, and Evie)

Daily you are tangible evidence of God's graciousness to me. Kaye, I am honored to be your husband. Eden and Evie, being your dad brings me great joy. I pray that I serve and lead you well.

Kevin

The Peck girls (Leslie, Ellie, Halle, and Ivey)

Leslie, your patience, love, and joy are a constant reminder of the grace of God in our home. Thank you for loving Jesus the way you do. Ellie, Halle, and Ivey, I am ever humbled to be your daddy. I know that God is shaping you each for a life that brings Him so much glory.

Acknowledgments

From Eric:

I am very grateful for the men and women I serve alongside on the leadership team of the Resources Division. You lead with "integrity of heart and skillful hands." It is an honor to serve the Church with you. I could never adequately repay Dr. Thom Rainer and Dr. Brad Waggoner (the CEO and Executive Vice President of LifeWay) for their investment and belief in me. I am thankful for Devin Maddox, our editor, for his passion for the Lord and the Church. That passion combined with a brilliance with words, a relentless work ethic, and understanding of publishing makes a project like this joyful and life-giving. Finally, it has been an honor to work with Kevin on this project. God has been very good to give me a friend like Kevin, a man who walks with the Lord, loves his family, and practices all we preach in this book.

From Kevin:

I am stunned at the grace God has given me in the leaders I am blessed to walk with. To Matt Carter, Halim Suh, Aaron Ivey, Dave Barrett, Todd Engstrom, James Paquette, Travis Wussow, John Manning, and Larry Cotton: I am daily strengthened by your love for Jesus and encouraged by your steadfast brotherhood. You men have made me a better pastor, husband, dad, leader, brother, and friend. I also must express my deepest thanks to the elders and church family at The Austin Stone Community Church. Their patience, kindness, and love have been a constant grace to me. I cannot imagine a better place to grow as a follower of Jesus and as a leader. My thanks also to Devin Maddox for his tireless work and tremendous skill in shaping this book. He is a true blessing to God's Church. And, finally, it has been a tremendous joy to work on this project with Eric Geiger. Eric truly makes much of Jesus by the way he leads his family, God's Church, and the LifeWay team. His friendship and leadership are immeasurable gifts to me in life and ministry.

CONTENTS

Conclusion

THE CHURCH AS A LEADERSHIP LOCUS

*Give me ten men that hate nothing but sin and love
nothing but God and we will change the world.*
—JOHN WESLEY

Where is the leadership locus in your community? In your town or city, where do leaders come from? Where are leaders formed, developed, and sent into the world? In your context, what group of people excels at creating leaders who impact the world?

Your church should be a leadership locus.

Locus can be defined as "a central or main place where something happens or is found." The locus of any activity is not on the fringes, but the core of where action happens. The locus is a strong concentration, the anchor, or the center of gravity. For example, when someone speaks of "locus of power," the reference is to a small group of people who call all the shots. When a news anchor speaks of the "locus of resistance" in an area of the world, the anchor is referring to the center of the fighting or rebelling.

Because the word *locus* indicates a strong center, many would deem "leadership locus" a misnomer. Because leadership is practiced in a plethora of environments, can there really be a locus? With all the wide range of leadership definitions and frameworks offered through leadership books, leadership podcasts, leadership coaches, and leadership classes, is there *really* such a thing as a leadership locus?

And if there is a center, can that center be the Church?[1]

If We Believe

The Church is uniquely set apart to develop and deploy leaders for the glory of God and the advancement of the gospel. The Church is designed by God to create leaders for all spheres of life. *Your* church is designed to lead, designed to disciple leaders who are, by God's grace, commanded to disciple people in all spheres of life. How can we make such a strong statement?

If we believe that apart from Him we can do nothing (John 15:5), we must recognize that much of what is recognized as "leadership" will not stand the test of time. In the end, all that is done apart from Him will be proven to be rubble and worth absolutely nothing. No matter how convincing modern wisdom may seem, apart from the wisdom and activity of God, all human leadership activity will prove futile in the end. Leadership, apart from the work of God, cannot produce true flourishing or eternal results.

If we believe that God created the world and handed responsibility for watching over the garden to Adam and Eve, then human leadership must be understood as God-initiated. He purposed to use humanity to steward and cultivate (Gen. 1—2); His people were and are "at the center" of His plan. From the beginning, His people have been designed to lead.

If we believe that God has chosen to make His multifaceted wisdom known through the Church (Eph. 3:10), then the leaders that are developed through the Church are "at the center" of God's design to represent Himself in all facets of life. Leaders who are motivated by His grace and shaped by His Word are leaders who invest their lives in what really matters.

If we believe, as William Temple stated, "The Church is the only society that exists for the benefit of those who are not its members," then all of humanity benefits from the leaders created and formed in the Church. No organization carries such a holy mandate, thus the leaders developed in the Church and by the Church are leaders who are developed for the world. They are developed "in the center" and sent out to the world. The world is impacted and improved by the leaders the Church develops and deploys.

If we believe that ultimately only Jesus transforms, then only the message the Church carries can bring about true, everlasting change. Only the gospel, the message His people steward, can change the human heart. And the leaders that the Church develops administer the grace of God in its various forms (1 Pet. 4:10).

If we believe the command to make disciples (Matt. 28:19) is bigger and more beautiful than merely making converts and calling people to "make a decision," then we understand the essential role of the Church in maturing people in Christ. The command to "make disciples" carries the connotation of forming believers who learn and develop over a lifetime.[2] One result, then, of discipleship is believers who serve and influence others in all spheres of life. The Great Commission is Plan A; Jesus has no Plan B. Discipleship, developing believers who grow over a lifetime, is His method. The full extent of discipleship is the development of disciples who are able to lead and develop others, not merely people who gather together for worship once a week.

So, yes, there is a locus of truly sustaining and transforming leadership. And the locus of leadership is the Church of Jesus Christ. She has been designed by God to develop and produce leaders who bless and serve others.

God's people are designed to influence others. God's people have been purchased by His blood and are empowered with His Spirit to influence the world around them. They are designed to lead. If you are His, you are designed to lead. And your church is designed to create and commission leaders who serve the world as they represent Christ and reconcile people to Him.

Notice we are not saying that the locus of the Church is leadership development, but that the locus of leadership development is the Church. Please do not miss the difference. The locus of the Church is and must be Jesus and His finished work for us. The center of the Church must be the gospel; for it is the gospel—His righteousness given to us in exchange for our sin—that created the Church, and it is the gospel that sustains the Church.

The center of the Church is the gospel, but the center of leadership development must be the Church—meaning, that the leaders who will ultimately transform communities and change the world come from the Church. These leaders carry with them, into all spheres of life and culture, the conviction of a people who are the *called-out ones*, of a people who have been brought from death to life through Jesus. These leaders are designed to serve others because they have been served first by Christ. These leaders are empowered to sacrificially offer themselves to others because their hearts have been transformed with the sacrifice of Jesus for us.

God has designed His people to lead. From the first recordings of history, God has made it clear that He has designed creation to be led by His covenant people. More than that, He has decided what His people are to do with that leadership. Whether you are called to lead your home, in the marketplace, in God's Church, or in your community—if you are called by God, then you are called to lead others to know and worship Jesus Christ.

Leadership: Go Forth and Die

Robert Quinn, a leadership professor at University of Michigan, has joined others in pointing out that the origins of the word *leader* means to "go forth and die."[3] In his book *Change the World*, he writes:

> Leadership authors do not understand that leadership means "Go forth to die." If they did understand it, they would not be enticed to write about it—because people do not want to hear this message. Most people want to be told how to get extraordinary results with minimum risk. They want to know how to get out-of-the-box results with in-the-box courage.[4]

True leaders are servants who die to themselves so others may flourish. True leaders go forth, not for themselves, but for others. The Church, as no other group, follows the only One to die that others may forever live. If the foundation of leadership is "go forth and die," then the Church must be the epicenter for developing and deploying these kinds of leaders. Who but the Church can really understand the weight and significance of "go forth and die"?

The Church has been served. The Church exists because our great death-defeating Savior went forth to die for us and, now, invites all who follow Him to die to themselves and truly live. The message of our Savior-King dying in our place is central, and of first importance, to believers. He went forth and endured the shame and pain of the cross for us. We are His because He served us.

The essence of Christianity is not that we serve Him first, but that He has served us by sacrificing Himself on the cross in our place and enduring our suffering and shame. On the cross He was treated as we deserve, so we may be treated as He deserves. His dying words capture the essence of the Christian faith: "It is finished!" (John 19:30). His sacrifice is final, the work is complete, and our salvation is secure.

Reportedly, Buddha's dying words were, "Strive without ceasing."[5] Work really hard for your own salvation! He died giving a pep talk, while our Savior died securing our redemption. No one has served the way Jesus has served us.

The Church has the ultimate example. His service to us is the example He has instructed us to emulate. Because He has served us, we are now free to "go forth and die" by serving others. After He washed His disciples' feet, Jesus said:

> "So if I, your Lord and Teacher, have washed your feet, you also ought to wash one another's feet. For I have given you an example that you also should do just as I have done for you." (John 13:14–15)

Jesus shows us that the values in His Kingdom are the opposite of the values in this world. In His Kingdom, the hungry are full, the poor are rich, the last are first, and "whoever wants to be great among you must become your servant" (Matt. 20:26).

The Christian life is about dying. When Jesus invited the crowd to follow Him, He invited them to die. When He told them His followers would be taking up their cross daily (Luke 9:23), they knew He meant a life of dying, as the cross was an explicit statement of death. The Christian life is not about trying daily, but dying daily. His life is revealed in us, with increasing measure, as we die to ourselves (2 Cor. 4:11). We grow by continually "going forth to die."

Christians, more than anyone else, should resonate with what it means to "go forth and die." Christians, more than anyone else, have been designed to lead. The Church, more than anyone else, is designed by God to create these kinds of leaders. No other people have been secured with the blood of Christ, knit together solely by His grace, and commissioned by Him to multiply. The Church has been providentially formed by God to bless the world, to be a holy gathering of people who make disciples. The Church has been designed to possess a holy rhythm of gathering people to scatter so more may be gathered.

Should Not Be Outpaced

Because the core of sustaining and transforming leadership is the Church, no organization should outpace the Church in developing leaders. *Why should we not be outpaced?* No other gathering of people has a greater mission, a greater promise, or a greater Reward.

No greater mission. Today, even as you read this, leaders are being recruited. There are meetings taking place around conference tables, over meals, and in coffee shops. Potential leaders are being asked to join a company, to give to a cause, or to join the core team of a start-up. In each of those meetings some type of mission is discussed.

Our company is really about this . . .

You can make a difference by giving to this . . .

Our start-up is going to do this . . .

If the one doing the inviting is wise, the "this" is a compelling and catalyzing mission. Any amount of time spent reading about leadership will tell you that you can't have a strong and committed team without a deep sense of mission. But any mission that people are being invited to join pales in comparison to the mission God has given His people. No other people have been reconciled to God through Christ and been given the privilege and responsibility to reconcile others to Christ. God's people are, therefore, His "ambassadors," and God makes His appeal to others through us (2 Cor. 5:20).

Because a local church exists to serve her community, to bless the world, and to be a light to the nations, then the leaders developed in each local church are developed for much more than each local church. In the church we are recruiting leaders to a mission bigger than the smaller ones the world offers. Whether we lead our homes, companies, or churches, our mission is always bigger than the organization we lead. As Christ-followers everything we lead can be used for His glory. Any and every organizational mission is trumped by the larger one the Lord has given His people: to make much of Jesus through our lives and to make disciples of all nations.

No greater promise. No one should outpace the Church in developing leaders because no one else has the assurance that their contribution will last, that their leadership will eternally matter. No other gathering of people will stand the test of time. Companies that have been declared successful are no longer in existence. Organizations falter as quickly as they rise.

Organizational theorists even plot out the typical life cycles of an organization from birth to growth to maturity to decline to death. The Church of Jesus Christ cannot be plotted on the chart. She cannot be contained! She will stand the test of time. Jesus has and will preserve His Church, and the gates of Hades will not overcome her (Matt. 16:18).

No greater reward. There is a great cost to following Jesus, and Jesus never minimized it. He taught the crowds that following Him means dying to ourselves and giving up everything to be His disciple (Luke 14:33). We discover that everything we give up is really nothing compared to the greatness of knowing Christ. The cost is great, but the reward is greater. We get Jesus. He is our great joy.

When Peter mentioned to Jesus that he and the other disciples had left everything to follow Jesus, Jesus responded:

> "I assure you, there is no one who has left house, brothers or sisters, mother or father, children, or fields because of Me and the gospel, who will not receive 100 times more, now at this time—houses, brothers and sisters, mothers and children, and fields, with persecutions—and eternal life in the age to come." (Mark 10:29–30)

No organization or opportunity offers what Jesus offers us. He promises us that the cost of work in His Kingdom will be worth it. Not only do we receive blessings and rewards, but above that He is our ultimate Reward, as everything is loss compared to the surpassing greatness of knowing Christ. Local churches should not be outpaced in developing leaders who bless the world and advance His Kingdom.

But . . .

But sadly many churches are outpaced in developing leaders for the mission of God. In many churches, leaders are not being developed as fully and intentionally as they could be. The lack of leadership development among God's people is the burden that has led to this book.

Your church should be, must be, a leadership locus.

Is it?

We wrote this book because we love the Church. But we also wrote this book with holy angst and anticipation for churches to excel in developing leaders who serve the world. Angst because our hearts grieve when ministry leaders fail to see the Kingdom potential in their midst, the "ordinary people" waiting to be developed and deployed. Anticipation because we have seen glimpses of churches who are centers of leadership, who disciple people to lead well in their homes, communities, businesses, and places of influence.

We long for your church to be a leadership locus, to embrace your design to lead.

In the next chapter, we are going to unpack a framework for developing leaders through your church. We say *through* because much of their Kingdom influence will happen outside the walls of your weekly gatherings. We want to offer you a framework to think about how leaders are formed and commissioned to impact the world. If leaders are not being developed in your context, this framework will help you identify what is missing. We will then spend the rest of the book unpacking the *Designed to Lead* framework.

What's Missing?

*Things which matter most must never be at
the mercy of things which matter least.*
—Wolfgang von Goethe

Developing leaders is hard work for an organization. It often seems like an even harder task for a local church. Many seem to be on the same page about its importance, and yet very few churches would admit to having a handle on the subject. Let us introduce you to three fictitious examples, though we could name dozens of real ones in each category.

Quitter Community Church (QCC): At QCC, the congregation has long existed in an ambivalent truce in the war of developing leaders. Congregants come to Sunday service and small group every week to learn about being a better Christian. The word *leader* at this church means volunteer with the job of doing whatever everyone else doesn't remember or want to do. Members with leadership skills outside the walls of the church are not expected to bring those skills to bear in the church because, well, "church is church" and "work is work" and "the two worlds don't need to intersect."

At QCC, the work of the church isn't a place for innovation, improvement, or creativity; it's a place for duty and faithfulness.

Duties are merely broken down into a manageable number of tasks and assigned to volunteers. Then the piles of tasks get too big for "just the volunteers"; the church looks at the budget and hires a new staff member according to their bylaws.

Church of the Flywheel: At the Flywheel, people know how to build things. A staff member brags, "Our system for making leaders is nails. We spent the last four years studying the most advanced leadership systems the world has to offer. We've studied the Armed Forces, Fortune 500s, and even several agencies in the espionage world." But alongside all their systems is one major problem . . . *no one cares.*

The plans are met with blank stares. The "pipelines" are empty. The slogans and nudges from the platform to "own your development" fall on deaf ears. Sure, a few months after each major overhaul and new emphasis the church always gets a new batch of Johnny-come-latelies to jump into the amazing system; but they always seem to flake out. The staff knows this is a problem and pontificates, "Our content and system is good; maybe we just have a congregation full of duds?" *Yeah, that's probably it.*

Talk Louder Community Church: Talk Louder claims to be all about making leaders. "Every year we have two sermon series on developing the next generation of leaders and we give everyone in the congregation the next best leadership book. It's a success every time! We have nearly 50 percent of our people who see themselves as having leadership potential, and most of them have signed up to volunteer. We have piles of people every year take a gifts profile, and most people look really promising." Still, strangely enough, every time there is a staff opening the leaders at Talk Louder have to look outside the body. And the truth is that those piles of "gift tests" sit on a desk, untouched since they were completed.

Also at Talk Louder, all the emphasis on "leadership" is focused on "making the church better." Though not explicitly stated this way, the emphasis of the church is essentially: "Come to our church, get plugged in, and volunteer to help us do church even better." Because of this, members at Talk Louder are no more likely to be effective leaders at home or in the marketplace than they were before joining the church. Thoughtful leaders on the team know this and struggle, "Every year we think we are taking big strides by creating more momentum for developing leaders, but something is holding us back from producing leaders." Something is missing at Talk Louder, and it isn't more rhetoric on leadership development.

Something is missing in many churches.

Perhaps you see your church in one of the examples. While fictitious, they are actually far too close and too real for many of us. It would be a challenge to find a vibrant evangelical church that doesn't admit that leadership development is a key function of the local church. And yet, it is our experience that very few church leaders can identify the problem that is hampering the leadership potential in their church. Church leaders know the people they serve have been made in His image, purchased with His blood, equipped with His Spirit, and called to make disciples, but they struggle with helping people live out the reality of their capacity to lead.

So the programmatic rat race in most churches continues. Most churches merely exist to keep running their programs and services. They are not developing leaders intentionally and consistently. When leaders emerge from some churches, it is often by accident. "Wow, a leader emerged. . . . How did *that* happen?" should not be heard among God's people. Something is missing. Something is off.

We attend conferences and preach sermons imploring the church of God to stand up and take hold of their destiny to advance the Kingdom of God across the globe. Still, our pews and folding chairs stay warm with immobile, uninspired, ill-equipped saints. Our churches, homes, and places of work lack the leadership of Christian men and women.

Something has to change.

We must find a way to unlock the power of God in the people of God, to see His sons and daughters rise up and lead for the glory of God. Jesus Himself has given to His blood-bought people the mandate to lead in His Kingdom, and to equip others to do the same.

For leaders to be developed consistently and intentionally, churches must possess *conviction, culture,* and *constructs*. Based on our own leadership and ministry experiences, studying leadership development, and interacting with churches and ministry leaders who develop others, we believe the following framework encompasses what must happen in a local church for leaders to be developed and deployed.

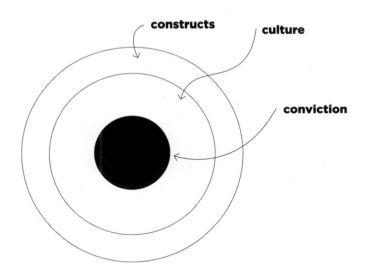

Designed to Lead Framework

Churches that consistently produce leaders have a strong *conviction* to develop leaders, a healthy *culture* for leadership development, and helpful *constructs* to systematically and intentionally build leaders. All three are essential for leaders to be formed through the ministry of a local church.

Conviction is a God-initiated passion that fuels a leader and church. Conviction is at the center of the framework because without conviction to develop others, leadership development will not occur. Developing leaders must be a burning passion, a non-negotiable part of the vision of a local church and her leaders, or it will never become a reality. The essential task of developing others must not be at the mercy of other things, of lesser things in a local church.

Once the church leaders share this conviction, this ambition must become part of the very *culture* of the church itself. *Culture* is the shared beliefs and values that drive the behavior of a group of people. The church that believes in and values the development of others collectively holds the conviction for leadership development. When development is in the culture, it is much more than an idea or program; it is part of the very core identity of the church.

Wise leaders implement *constructs* to help unlock the full potential of a church that seeks to be a center for developing leaders. By constructs, we mean the systems, processes, and programs developed to help develop leaders. Constructs provide necessary implementation and execution to the vision and passion of culture and conviction.

Because we have a proclivity to run to the practical for a quick fix and to find something we can quickly implement, most leaders will run to constructs when addressing leadership development problems in a church. While constructs are important, if you embrace and implement constructs without first developing a coherent and strong conviction and culture, you will only reap apathy or exhaustion.

Constructs without Conviction = Apathy. The reason that many people in churches give blank stares to leadership development initiatives is because an overarching sense of conviction has not been fostered in the church. The reason many churches settle for enlisting people to "fill necessary slots" to pull off programs is there is not a conviction for developing leaders. The pastors, the people, everyone has given up on the grand idea of discipling and deploying leaders. If a shared sense of conviction that God wants to raise up and release leaders in His Kingdom through His Church is lacking, apathy is sure to follow. If you want to know why churches have given up, look no further than lack of conviction.

Constructs without Culture = Exhaustion. Constructs are doomed to fail without strong conviction and a healthy culture. If a church attempts to execute constructs without a culture of leadership development, the systems will feel exhausting. The church longs for the "leadership flywheel" and seeks it through systems; but without a healthy culture those systems are merely seen as another set of things to do, a cumbersome hoop to jump through. And as staff attempts to implement, everyone grows weary. Every time the team aims to fill the leadership pipeline it feels as if they are pushing a boulder up a hill. An unhealthy culture breeds exhaustion.

Conviction without Constructs = Frustration. At the same time, if a team holds a deep conviction for development but lacks constructs to help develop leaders, frustration festers. Constructs are vitally important. Conviction and culture must be the starting point; but if constructs are not provided, then intentional and ongoing leadership development is merely wishful thinking. A vision without a strategy is nothing more than a fun whiteboard moment that rarely results in anything significant. There is nothing more frustrating than an unrealized vision, than a passion without any traction. A leader who isn't passionate about leadership development will sleep better tonight than the one who is but lacks necessary constructs to help develop leaders. A leader without constructs often says, "We keep talking (louder and louder) about developing leaders, but nothing happens."

Formulas for Diagnosis

Constructs without Conviction = Apathy

If a leader is apathetic, it could be they lack a proper sense of conviction.

Constructs without Culture = Exhaustion

If a leader is exhausted, it could be they are not a part of a healthy leadership culture.

Conviction without Constructs = Frustration

If a leader is frustrated, it could be they lack the constructs that are necessary to realize vision.

Conviction, culture, and constructs. If any of the three are missing, leadership development will be stifled. Is one missing in your context? Does one or more need focus and attention?

To further explain and illustrate the importance of all three, let's look at Moses and his leadership of God's people. Moses is as an example of a godly leader who developed others for the mission the Lord had for His people. In observing Moses' leadership, we can see a holy *conviction* for investing in others, an emphasis on a *culture* that develops leaders, and *constructs* that enables development.

Moses and Conviction

Often our churches don't make leaders because we lack conviction. Granted, it's probably much more than that, but it is certainly not less. If we look at Moses and Joshua, his successor, we see conviction for development in one and lacking in the other. And we also see that the implications of possessing or lacking a conviction for development are massive.

Conviction for developing others gripped Moses. He under-stood that leadership is always a temporary assignment—always. It is a temporary assignment because leaders do not ultimately own the teams, ministries, or organizations they lead. We simply steward what the Lord has entrusted to our care for a season. The brevity of life ought to birth urgency in us to develop others. Not to mention that our time in this life is much more limited than that of Moses! He lived to be 120 and lived with an urgency to develop others; how much more should we embrace the temporary nature of our time as leader? Part of wise and selfless stewardship is developing others and preparing them for their impending time to lead.

Moses personally selected and invested in leaders. As you read through the Scripture, you see Moses pouring into Joshua. Moses brought Joshua up the mountain to receive the Ten Commandments from God (Exod. 24:13). Joshua observed Moses' righteous indig-nation when Moses smashed the two tablets (Exod. 32:17–19), and Joshua sensed the sweet communion Moses shared with the Lord as Joshua guarded the Tent of Meeting (Exod. 33:11). Joshua was also chosen to spot out the land of Canaan.

Through all these critical moments in the life of God's people, Joshua was there with Moses. Moses served God's people by pour-ing into the life of another. And immediately after Moses' death, Joshua was ready to lead Israel.

> After the death of Moses the LORD's servant, the LORD spoke to Joshua son of Nun, who had served Moses: "Moses My servant is dead. Now you and all the people prepare to cross over the Jordan to the land I am giving the Israelites." (Josh. 1:1–2)

The leadership legacy of Joshua, sadly, is very different:

> Joshua son of Nun, the servant of the LORD, died at the age of 110. . . . That whole generation was also gathered to their

ancestors. After them another generation rose up who did not know the LORD or the works He had done for Israel. (Judg. 2:8, 10)

Did you notice the significant difference in the legacies of Moses and Joshua? After Moses died, immediately God's people were ready to move to the land the Lord had given them. After Joshua died, a generation rose up who did not even know what the Lord had done for His people. Why the stark contrast?

There is no record of Joshua investing in anyone. We don't see him intentionally developing leaders. We don't read of him pouring into others. And the generation after his leadership doesn't know the Lord. Israel enters a period marked by leadership failure after leadership failure. We know this period as it is recorded in the book of Judges. The book opens with the people of Israel asking God who should go first, who should lead them. There was no clear leader out in front. From this moment, leader after leader steps up and leads more poorly than the last. Because of Joshua's shortsightedness, Israel is in a leadership crisis.

Clearly Joshua lacked the conviction to develop others. Even still, as most leaders, he likely would never have admitted that. He would have claimed developing leaders was a priority, something that was important to him, but his life over the long haul revealed it wasn't.

Over time, our lives, not merely our words, reveal our convictions. And based on the lack of leadership development in many of our churches, it is clear that many church leaders lack a real conviction for developing leaders.

How do you know if something is a conviction? If you can imagine life or ministry without it, it is *not* a conviction. For example, we are deeply encouraged that most church leaders hold a conviction that Jesus must be preached, that there is salvation in no other name but Jesus. Because Jesus is a conviction, ministry leaders cannot fathom ministry without preaching and teaching Jesus.

Amen! If someone offered these leaders a more "successful" or "larger" ministry if they didn't preach Jesus, they would refuse. No way they would even consider it. Their response would be: "What's the point if Jesus isn't the focus? Who cares if tons of people gather around something else other than Jesus?" This is conviction.

Or take evangelism as an example. If a leader was assured that an easier ministry awaits if "you never challenge people to share their faith, to engage people who are not Christians, and to be salt and light in their communities," the leader who holds firmly to a conviction that Christians are commanded to share the gospel would never take the route of an easier ministry. It would be unthinkable because evangelism *is* a conviction.

Clearly most church leaders do not hold the conviction of developing leaders, so they find ways to continue in ministry without it. They have learned to lead churches without developing leaders. They have learned to offer programs, conduct worship services, and manage budgets all without developing leaders. Like Joshua, they are able to execute tasks and make decisions without any conviction to develop leaders. It is to our shame that we have learned to lead ministries without developing other ministers.

Are you more like Moses or Joshua? Does a conviction for developing leaders grip your heart? Or can you actually function and see your church function without it?

Moses and Culture

Culture bridges conviction and constructs. If a church has a strong culture of development, it was birthed from conviction. And a church with a strong culture of developing and deploying leaders will keep working to find or build constructs that help them develop leaders.

Leaders must own the culture of the ministry they are leading. A seminary professor once shared, "You can complain about the culture of your ministry your first three years, but after that it is a reflection of your leadership." By culture, we are not speaking of the socioeconomic or ethnic makeup of the ministry you lead, but the shared beliefs and values that undergird all your church does. Thus a strong culture of developing leaders permeates the entire church.

Culture is powerful. It constantly teaches, constantly shapes, and constantly forms the people who are within it. Peter Drucker famously said, "Culture eats strategy for breakfast." He was not diminishing the role of strategy or systems. He advocated for their use, but it is possible to have the right systems and a great strategy in the midst of an unhealthy culture. And if the culture is not healthy, the unhealthy culture swallows the systems and strategies.

As Moses led God's people, there was the famous confrontation between Jethro and Moses in Exodus 18. Jethro visited his son-in-law Moses and observed that Moses was worn out by the magnitude of the responsibility. So he confronted Moses with the truth, "What you're doing is not good" (v. 17), and challenged him to delegate responsibilities to others. But in the midst of the encouragement to delegate, Jethro tells Moses that there are several things he must do—several things he must not delegate. Don't miss this: In the midst of the famous delegation passage, Jethro tells Moses there are things he must not delegate. And the things "Moses must do" are all essential in building a healthy culture of development.

> "Instruct them about the statutes and laws, and teach them the way to live and what they must do. But you should select from all the people able men, God-fearing, trustworthy, and hating bribes. Place them over the people as commanders of thousands, hundreds, fifties, and tens." (Exod. 18:20–21)

The responsibilities that Jethro encourages Moses to retain are culture-forming responsibilities. *Instruct* them about the statutes and laws; provide clarity about their identity. *Teach* them the way to live; provide focus of mission. *Select* the leaders; provide leaders for the people. In a healthy culture, the people know who they are, what they are to do, and leaders are being developed and deployed. In a healthy culture there is strong sense of identity, clarity of mission, and credible leaders with integrity.

A healthy culture has a strong identity. Jethro confronted Moses in Exodus 18, and in Exodus 20, God gave His people the Law. So before the Law was even given, Jethro encouraged Moses to "instruct the people in the statutes of God."

God gave the Law, in part, to show us we can't keep the Law—that we need Jesus. Also He gave the Law to form a distinct people who would be a blessing to all other peoples. God was using the laws and statues that Moses would constantly teach to form His people to be a kingdom of priests and a holy and distinct nation (Exod. 19:6). They were His prized possession, distinct from all other nations to be a blessing to all other nations. The Law reminded the people of their God, of His great rescue, of His great adoption of them. As God gives the Ten Commandments two chapters later, He reminds them, "I am the LORD your God, who brought you out of the land of Egypt, out of the place of slavery" (Exod. 20:2).

A healthy leadership culture doesn't allow for tasks and assignments to be merely handed to people without connecting the responsibilities to the identity God's people have as sons, daughters, and servants of our King. In a healthy culture, people are continually reminded who they are, that they are His people, rescued by Him, a royal priesthood, and a people belonging to Him. If people are not reminded of their identity, they will be burdened with lists of tasks and responsibilities without their hearts being refreshed and renewed by the Lord who loves them.

More important than work getting done is the Lord's refreshing work in the hearts of His people. Jethro was the "org design guy," and even he challenged Moses to first and foremost instruct the people in their distinction. If we forget who we are, we mindlessly execute and perform ministry functions without the sacred *why* behind all our actions.

A healthy culture has a clear mission. Jethro also encouraged Moses to "teach them the way to live, and what they must do" (Exod. 18:20). Not only were God's people to understand their unique identity, but also they were to receive instructions on "how we live around here." They were given a sense of mission as God's people.

Michael Goheen reminds us that "the Great Commission is not a task assigned to isolated individuals; it is an identity given to a community."[1] Jesus didn't simply ransom a random collection of individuals; rather He purchased a new community, a special people. This people, whom He named the Church, are called, not only *to God*, but *for God's glory*. We are, at our very core, a missional people. This reality is the basic understanding of the identity of the New Testament church. It's the culture of the new Kingdom under Christ. Because He has redeemed us, we join Him in His mission to bring redemption to others. The mission of God is for the people of God.

You can't have a strong culture without a strong sense of mission. A healthy ministry cultivates a clear sense of "here is what we are going to do together." Jim Collins wrote that when an "organization has a strong vision, a sense of why they are here, a visitor could drop in from another planet and understand the vision without having to read it on paper."[2]

A local church with a strong sense of mission will inevitably invite and develop others to join the mission. The mission is too important, too overwhelming to attempt alone. Thus churches with a deep burden for their cities or a passion for unreached people groups will attract leaders and develop them through the mission and for the mission.

Ministries without a clear sense of mission move in a plethora of directions, as a multitude of lesser and competing missions invade the culture. In a world of complex and competing causes and messages, we must be ruthlessly committed to the mission of making disciples. Thus a church's mission statement should be more than merely, "Come to our church, get connected, and help us do church better." What an incomplete mission and a shallow view of discipleship! We are the people of God, the called-out ones. Those outside of us should benefit from our existence, from our community, from our gatherings.

A healthy culture develops and deploys godly leaders. While Jethro encouraged Moses to delegate responsibility to others, he also challenged Moses to be personally involved in the selection and placement of leaders.

> "Select from all the people able men, God-fearing, trust-worthy, and hating bribes. Place them over the people as commanders of thousands, hundreds, fifties, and tens." (Exod. 18:21)

Moses was tasked with selecting and placing leaders of both character and competence so that the people would be served well. Those selected and placed were to be God-fearing, trustworthy, and able. Jethro emphasized God-fearing and trustworthy because the culture among God's people was going to be set by the character of those in leadership.

The leaders who have responsibility entrusted to them dramatically shape the culture of any ministry or organization. The health of a culture is deeply connected to the health of her leaders. Leaders shape the ministry culture infinitely more than your policies or programs.

With Jethro-like intensity, when the apostle Paul challenged Timothy to expand the ministry and reproduce himself in others, he emphasized trustworthiness. He didn't diminish competence, but he started with integrity and faithfulness. The apostle Paul told the young pastor, Timothy:

> What you have heard from me in the presence of many witnesses entrust to faithful men who will be able to teach others also. (2 Tim. 2:2 ESV)

Notice the order of the language of this often-quoted verse. The verse does not read, "Entrust to able men who will be faithful." Paul is not saying: "Go find some great leaders and try to make them faithful. Make a list of high-capacity leaders and work to turn them into faithful followers. Find the best, most talented people and put them through a character boot camp."

To the contrary, Paul essentially says, "Entrust all the important things to the faithful, and in time, they will be able." Though the temptation is to find anyone to "fill a spot," Paul is saying the opposite:

> Find those whose hearts are His and coach them on their competence.

> Invest in people who love the Lord and develop their skills.

> Pour yourself into people who have devoted themselves to Him.

Biblical leadership development is to "find the faithful who will be able. Not the able that might be faithful." Reversing the order of the famous leadership development verse may provide short-term relief, but it has massive long-term implications. Undoubtedly you have seen the devastating effects of character implosion in ministry leaders, whether prominent leaders or those who serve in less visible roles. Regardless the situation, when the role and responsibility outpace the leader's character, disaster is inevitable. And more people than the leader suffer.

Entrusting leadership to the faithful, to the God-fearing, does not mean entrusting leadership to those who are sinless, as there is only One. Being a person of integrity isn't about perfection, but it is about the direction of one's heart. Someone who is faithful repents, displays the fruit of the Spirit, and lives a life directionally in submission to the Lord, not directionally in opposition to the Lord.

Oswald Sanders stated strongly, "Spiritual leadership requires Spirit-filled people."[3] Spirit-filled leaders are required to lead a ministry that produces other Spirit-filled leaders. If our churches are developing leaders who are not filled with His Spirit, our churches are developing leaders who will not advance the mission and serve the Kingdom well. When a church produces leaders apart from the Spirit, a church produces people who can execute tasks without walking with the Lord, who can fulfill responsibilities without remaining in Him. Without Spirit-filled people, all the work that gets done, all the energy that gets expended, and all the activity that fills schedules and calendars amounts to nothing in the end. For apart from Him, we can do absolutely nothing. Thus a healthy culture—a culture that produces spiritual leaders—values the character and trustworthiness of the leaders, not merely the skills they can offer.

The world benefits from leaders who are surrendered to the Spirit, men and women whose character is formed by the Lord. According to research conducted by KRW International, CEOs noted for their integrity led their organizations to higher levels of performance than those CEOs with lower integrity scores.[4] Employees were asked to rate their CEOs on integrity, responsibility, forgiveness, and compassion. And those CEOs with higher marks led their companies to higher returns as compared to the CEOs with lower marks. *The Harvard Business Review* article that reported the research declared, "The people who work for you will benefit from the tone you set. And now there's evidence that your company will too."[5] The world is longing for leaders who are filled with integrity, responsibility, forgiveness, and compassion. In essence, even the world's research says that the world benefits from leadership that is Christian in nature.

Without faithful men and women, a ministry culture loses credibility. The ministry may produce great programs, be well-managed, and meet budget, but if the leaders lack character, the ministry lacks the moral authority and credibility to call others to come and die, to challenge men and women to become leaders.

In their landmark leadership book *The Leadership Challenge*, Jim Kouzes and Barry Posner articulate that the most important leadership characteristic is credibility. Of credibility they write:

> Credibility is one of the hardest attributes to earn. And it's the most fragile of human qualities. It's earned minute-by-minute, hour-by-hour, month-by-month, year-by-year. But it can be lost in very short order if not attended to. We're willing to forgive a few minor transgressions, a slip of the tongue, a misspoken word, a careless act. But there comes a time when enough is enough. And when leaders have used up all of their credibility, it's nearly impossible to earn it back.[6]

Ministry leadership often requires leaders and teams to take risks and make bold moves. But wise leaders in a healthy culture don't risk the credibility of the ministry by placing unfaithful and untrustworthy leaders into roles. A healthy culture that values leadership development has a strong identity, a clear sense of mission, and is committed to selecting and deploying godly leaders.

Moses and Constructs

In looking at Moses' leadership, we see someone who held a conviction to develop others. And we see how Jethro's instructions to Moses, the things he told him not to delegate, were instrumental in developing the culture among God's people. But we also see the wise counsel of Jethro insisting that Moses build a leadership system, a *construct* that would serve God's people.

"Place them over the people as commanders of thousands, hundreds, fifties, and tens. They should judge the people at all times. Then they can bring you every important case but judge every minor case themselves. In this way you will lighten your load, and they will bear it with you. If you do this, and God so directs you, you will be able to endure, and also all these people will be able to go home satisfied." (Exod. 18:21–23)

Before Jethro arrived, there was confusion and chaos. People waited all day to see Moses. He went home exhausted. Decisions were delayed that could have been made. Actions that should have been taken were put on hold until Moses could review plans and give his ruling.

Without constructs, without systems, chaos and confusion always abound.

Before Jethro's counsel, Moses delegated responsibilities to himself. If there had been an org chart, Moses would have been in every box. If a task needed to get done, Moses would be the one to do it. He was the superstar leader who attempted to meet every need and do all the ministry himself as the people watched. He needed to repent of his foolish attempts to be omni-competent, and Jethro provided the appropriate rebuke. No leader is omni-competent. The beauty of the body of Christ is that we need one another. For a pastor, or the people in a church, to view a pastor as omni-competent is to insult the body of Christ. "The body is not one part but many" (1 Cor. 12:14). All of God's people are part of the body of Christ with an important function, an important role.[7]

More than just offering a rebuke, Jethro instructed Moses to build a leadership system, to design and architect a structure that will distribute the responsibility to others so that the people will receive care. And if you do this, Jethro told Moses, the "people will go home satisfied" (NIV). Meaning, the motivation was not merely for Moses to have a lighter load, but also so the people would be better served.

Building constructs, delegating and broadening the capacity of the ministry, is not *only* about the leaders having a lighter load. The burden will be lighter and the pace will be more sustainable, but the people will also go home satisfied. And though Jethro was a priest of Midian—meaning, he was not a Jew but an outsider—Moses listened to him because the counsel was wise. Moses designed a system, placed leaders in significant areas of responsibility, and delegated both responsibility and authority. The system was a tool to organize and deploy leaders so that the people of God would be better served.

For any organization to develop and deploy lots of leaders, constructs are required. Quite simply, leadership development cannot be scaled without systems that undergird the development of leaders. A leadership construct provides a framework for leadership development, a pipeline for future leaders, and a path for people to walk in their own leadership development.

Ultimately, the development of leaders within the church serves as a locus for developing leaders for places of leadership all over the world. Leadership constructs should not only result in leaders developed for ministry within a church, but also for leadership in the home, workplace, and world. The Church is able to multiply the Christ-empowered leaders the world desperately needs.

So we say it again: your church, the one you worship with every Sunday, is divinely designed to develop leaders who will bless and serve their families, churches, communities, and the world. But conviction, culture, and constructs are all required. Without them your church may offer programs, fill calendars, exist with an array of activity, and may even fill all your volunteer spots, but you won't develop leaders the way God intended.

Let's Go . . .

We don't want to be overly dramatic, but there is so much at stake here. The Church of God must be the locus of leadership development that God has designed her to be. As we struggle to find traction in this climb to our destiny, so much of the world around us is suffering from the lack of God's leaders. The world is in agony awaiting the leadership of God through the people of God. We must not give up, and we cannot abdicate our duty. There is a way forward, but local churches must pursue this endeavor with diligence and determination. Our churches must preach and teach this conviction until our cultures bleed it. But we cannot stop there. Our passion must turn to action through thoughtful constructs.

Perhaps as you are reading this book, you yourself are in a situation like Quitter Community Church; the dream and conviction of developing world-changing leaders has been assigned to legend and mythology. Or maybe you are in a context like Church of the Flywheel; you have systems without a culture, systems without an identity. Or maybe you resonate with the people at Talk Louder Community Church; there are no constructs to undergird all the messages.

There is no doubt that the work of leadership development is hard. But it is no mere work of fiction . . . God's Church was designed to lead. To develop leaders, you must have a strong *conviction*, a healthy *culture*, and simple *constructs*. We are going to walk through all three in the following chapters. Let's go . . .

Conviction

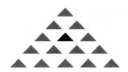

"Without conviction, leadership development will not occur. Developing leaders must be a burning passion, a nonnegotiable part of the vision of a local church and her leaders, or it will never become a reality."

HOLY CAUSE AND EFFECT: THE CONVICTION FOR LEADERSHIP

*If the pastor is a superstar, the church
is an audience, not a body.*
—HOWARD SNYDER

We have five daughters, and no sons, between us, so we are adept at executing ponytails, discussing princesses, and painting pottery. We have vacationed together several times, meaning we have waited in lines together for hours at Disney World to secure a signature from a princess, and our wives have scolded us, "Slow down, they are little girls" when driving a boat with our daughters trailing behind on a big tube. Fathering girls is different than anything we have ever done, and we both love it.

On our best days, we embrace the enormity of the responsibility with eyes toward the future. We are helping prepare our girls for life outside our homes. Our time with them is short, and it is moving so fast. Our role is not to keep them in our homes forever. Our role is to not to help them live out the Christian faith only when they are safe in our presence, but also in our absence. One day, we won't bring them to work like we bring them to school.

One day, we won't make all the choices for them that we are making now. Our role is to equip them, not to feverishly attempt to live their lives for them.

Leading people in a local church is very similar. Leaders, when embracing the enormity of the responsibility, keep an eye on the future. They develop others, not just for the comfort of life in the church, but also for life as a whole. They equip God's people to serve, not feverishly attempting to do all the ministry themselves. Both parenting and pastoring must focus on equipping.

Two major problems are plaguing many churches. If you read a book directed toward church leaders, likely one of these problems will be lamented. If you attend a conference for ministry leaders, you will inevitably hear wise and gifted speakers tackle one of these problems. But usually, you will not hear both problems addressed in relation to one another. These are the two problems: (1) many churches are not healthy, and (2) churches, in general, struggle to equip people for ministry.

Many churches are not healthy. A plethora of symptoms are lamented, from a lack of generosity to low ministry engagement to the scarcity of God's people living on mission. Symptoms are often addressed, but the symptoms point to an overarching sickness. For example, a lack of generosity reveals a loss of awe for His generosity, that He who was rich became poor for us. The scant number of people, in most churches, who view their neighborhoods and professions as God-given mission opportunities, reveals an incomplete view of or lack of passion for the mission of God. The examples of symptoms could continue, and they painfully remind us that many local churches are not as healthy as they could and should be.

Churches, in general, struggle to equip people for ministry. In a recent research project, pastors were surveyed and asked questions about their church's plan for developing and training people for ministry.[1] Less than 25 percent of church leaders said they had any semblance of a plan. Essentially the vast majority of churches admit they have *absolutely no* strategy for developing the people in their churches for ministry. Clearly, equipping others is a missing conviction in churches. Yet the apostle Paul wrote to the church in Ephesus:

> And He personally gave some to be apostles, some prophets, some evangelists, some pastors and teachers, for the training of the saints in the work of ministry, to build up the body of Christ, until we all reach unity in the faith and in the knowledge of God's Son, growing into a mature man with a stature measured by Christ's fullness. (Eph. 4:11–13)

Paul's exhortation is clear. When pastors/teachers train and prepare God's people for ministry, the result is the body of Christ is built up.

These two problems are interconnected. The scarcity of healthy churches and the lack of passion and plan to train people for ministry are not unrelated problems. In fact—according to the apostle Paul—one is the result of the other. Quite simply, a failure to equip people for ministry results in an unhealthy church. A lack of conviction for equipping results in an immature body of believers.

Holy Cause and Effect

Our lives are filled with the principle of "cause and effect." Doctors remind us that if we eat healthy, the effect will be a more healthy body. Dermatologists scold us that if we fail to use sunscreen, the effect will be damaging to our skin. Children are taught the principle early in elementary school because it is so critical to learning to make wise choices throughout life. But somehow many church leaders have missed the holy cause and the glorious effect that is clearly prescribed in Scripture.

There is a holy *cause and effect* in ministry. If we will make the training of the saints our holy cause, the effect is a healthy church.

A healthy church is not a perfect church, but she is a church that is being collectively formed more and more into the image of Christ. Paul writes that as the training of the saints in the work of the ministry occurs, a church will be growing "into a mature man with a stature measured by Christ's fullness."

To assert causation is to make a major claim. Researchers are typically very careful when they reveal significant research findings to say, "There is a significant relationship between . . ." so as not to be accused of implying that one thing causes another. For example, Eric has had to carefully state "relationship" and not "causation" on the church ministry books that have been developed out of large research projects. It is one thing to say, "There is a significant relationship between equipping believers and the health of a church," and quite another to say, "Equipping people makes a church healthy." The former statement positions "equipping believers" as one of many things that is present in healthy churches, as one of the observable characteristics in a healthy church. The latter statement boldly claims, "If you will equip believers, you will have a healthy church."

We are joining the apostle Paul in making the latter statement; to have a healthy church, a church must equip believers. We are not hedging. We are not merely suggesting that equipping people is important. We are not merely suggesting there is a relationship between equipping and health. We are declaring that equipping causes health. Equipping is the work of leadership.

Equipping must not be something that is seen as optional, something seen as for "other churches." It must be a deeply held conviction. Equipping is not just for the mega-church "who has resources to make that happen." It is not only for the new church "who can start with that in her DNA." It is not solely for the church in the city "who is filled with intellectuals who expect that." It is not merely for the rural church "who is filled with people who have more respect for church and less of a commute."

It is not only for the church with lots of programs "because they can easily add that to the agenda." It is not limited to the church with few programs "because they have time and space." Equipping is for every single church.

Equipping must be for your church.

Equipping must be viewed as foundational, as fundamental to what it means to actually be called a church.

The Cause

"You had one job" is a popular and sarcastic online catchphrase usually associated with blunders people have made while performing their jobs.[2] Examples include pictures of misspelled signage (frie instead of fire, shcool instead of school), a medal designed for the "3st place" winner, and "extinct" being featured in the "X" page of a children's alphabet book. The point of the memes is *"You had one job to do, Mr. sign painter, medal designer, and editor. Could you not do the one job, the one task, well?"*

The reality is we all fall woefully short, even if we focus on only one thing. And thankfully Jesus does not and will not shame us. Instead He takes all our sin and shame, gives us all His perfection, and views us as if we have always performed perfectly and obeyed Him joyfully.

But, according to this passage, pastors really do have one overarching job. God has given pastors to His Church, and their overarching job is "to equip the saints [God's people] for the work of the ministry" (Eph. 4:12 ESV). Equipping encompasses preaching/teaching (1 Tim. 3:2) and leading/governing (1 Tim. 3:4–5), as the goal in all of healthy ministry is to prepare or train God's people.[3] In fact, the Ephesians 4 passage is the only time the term "pastor" is used in the Bible to describe a human role or office. The terms *elder* and *bishop* are used other times to refer to the same office/role, but it is painfully ironic that the biblical term we most use (pastor) is connected to the practice we most often neglect (equipping).

Sadly many churches do not recognize or act on the assignment God has given pastors. For example, peruse the typical job descriptions churches give for their pastors. In many churches, you will likely find little emphasis on equipping people for ministry. According to the job descriptions, programs will be run and budgets will be managed but people may *or* may not be developed.

As another example, notice the list of responsibilities a church that is looking for a pastor will offer potential pastors. You can understand how the lengthy list is developed. A team tasked with the responsibility of finding the new pastor surveys the congregation for insights into what qualities the people feel are most important. When the responses are combined, you will find the church desires someone who is a great preacher, excellent with young families, wise in administration, a strong mentor for the staff, passionate for global missions, deeply connected in the local community, skilled in counseling, eager to visit the hospitals, innovative but not wanting to change things, and evangelistic of the kinds of people who are just like us. Oh yeah—and the pastor should be married with kids and fall squarely into the age range of the median household in the community.

When you read one of those lists you may think, *Wow. This church is actually looking for Jesus to be the pastor.* Except Jesus was not married with kids, so Jesus would not meet the qualifications some churches list when looking for a pastor.

Another thing stands out: many churches do not even list, on their very long list of pastoral profiles, equipping or training the people for ministry. And of the few churches that do, most have the responsibility so buried amongst the plethora of other tasks that it is unlikely to receive much attention. According to pastoral job descriptions and pastor search team profiles, the one job emphasized by Paul in Ephesians 4:11–12 is seldom "a job" and rarely "the job."

Prepare, Not Perform

There is a typical approach to local church ministry, and then there is the biblical approach. The typical approach to ministry in many churches looks like this:

pastors ➡ **minister** ➡ **people**

Typically pastors or other staff persons are hired to minister to people. The number of children in the church increases, so the solution is another staff person. The number of sick people is on the rise; therefore, someone is hired to visit the hospitals. The number of counseling appointments increases, so another part-time staff member is added. The system makes sense, really. People come to church and generously give money. So as the church grows, there is more money that can be given to compensate ministers—so church members, if a church is not careful, can subtly be taught that they are paying people to do ministry. And pastors and staff can place on themselves a burden to earn their pay by performing ministry well.

While the typical approach to ministry makes sense, it is deeply detrimental. The spiritual growth of the people in the body is hampered. People who are gifted by God and called to serve Him are put on the bench as they watch the "professional ministers" or the newest staff member make the ministry happen. They miss the joy of serving. And instead of fostering a serving posture among believers, the typical approach to ministry helps develop consumers and moochers rather than participants and contributors.

The typical approach to ministry also wrongly and implicitly teaches that church is "spiritual" and led by ministers only, which means the work of the regular folks must be second-class and "secular." So not only are people not developed for ministry within the church, they are also subtly taught to not even consider their "secular jobs" as places of Kingdom leadership.

The typical approach also hampers the movement of the church. The effectiveness of a local church is greatly slowed as people are taught that the majority of ministry occurs through the "professionals." The scope of the ministry, therefore, is limited to the time and abilities of a few people.

The biblical approach looks very different:

pastors ➡ prepare ➡ people ➡ minister ➡ each other

Pastors, and churches, with a biblical approach to ministry possess a deep-seated conviction that all believers are gifted for ministry, not just the "professionals." The Scripture never uses the term "minister" to set aside a special class of people who serve other Christians. *All believers are ministers.* Thus those selected by the Lord to be pastors are to invite all believers to engage in ministry and view themselves as equippers of all the ministers, all of God's people, within the Church.

God is deeply passionate for His Church, for His bride, and ferociously committed to maturing her. For this reason, "He personally gave some to be . . . pastors and teachers" (Eph. 4:11). He personally involves Himself in the process of setting apart pastors, not to *do* the ministry, but to prepare God's people.

Distinction versus Division

Perhaps an unbiblical approach to ministry exists in many churches because an inaccurate vocabulary has infiltrated the people of God. When most people hear terms like "clergy" and "laypeople," certain images and definitions enter their minds. And these definitions are often far from their original meaning.

Clergy. Churches often think it makes sense to hire clergy to do ministry because many believe that "the clergy" are a select group of people—a group able to offer spiritual counsel and insights that mere mortals could never; a group able to care for others in ways regular, everyday Christians could not. There are even "clergy parking" spots at hospitals, and we admit that we have taken advantage of the offer, but solely for opportunistic and practical reasons and not because we theologically believe in such a thing. After all, the term *clergy* comes from the Greek word *kleros* and refers to one's inheritance or a lot. So the sign in front of the best parking spots at the hospital literally means "inheritance parking."

In the Bible the word *kleros* does not refer to a select group of people who "do all the ministry." The opposite is true. The term actually applies to all believers who are "qualified . . . to share in the inheritance [the *kleros*] of the saints" (Col. 1:12 ESV). All Christians are ministers, and all Christians will share in the inheritance. The word was never intended to help foster a group of super Christians who do the ministry. In reality, the clergy parking spot is for all of us. But we accept no responsibility for your towing if you choose to grab an empty clergy spot.

Laypeople. "Oh, but I am not a pastor. I am just a layperson." We have heard that statement countless times when speaking to committed Christians at conferences or other events. Often the statement comes from someone who wants to serve God more, wants to lead and make an impact, but feels second class and unable to do anything really significant. The person is often searching for a bigger view of life and the mission of God, but the lie that ministry is for the professionals has been reinforced for years.

In the Scripture, the term *lay* comes from the Greek word *laos* and simply refers to God's special people. The *laos* are, therefore, not less significant. They are God's special people, those He has adopted as His own. All of us are "a royal priesthood, a holy nation, a people [*laos*] for His possession" (1 Pet. 2:9).

Biblically both terms apply to believers. We are all *laos*, people of His possession, and we all enjoy the *kleros*, the inheritance, as children of God. Literally, your pastor is a layperson and you share in the clergy.

Clergy and *laity* have been terms inaccurately used to create an unhealthy, unhelpful, and unbiblical division in the Church. The people of God are split in two, the "holy clergy" and the "lay-people" who tolerate work in unspiritual professions so they can pay the clergy to do the spiritual work. But this must not be; there should be no division in the body of Christ. The gospel creates a new humanity, a group of believers who are one because of Christ's atoning sacrifice for us (Gal. 3:25–27). We can't stand before Him in our race, status, gender, or profession. We are only qualified to stand before Him in His righteousness, which He has freely given us. And it is His righteousness that unites us and tears down divisions. Of no divisions, Edmund Clowney beautifully wrote:

> Spiritual dominion by princes of the church is doubly impossible: Christ the king is with his people; his people are kings with Christ. Can any officer outrank an "ordinary" Christian who shares Christ's throne and will judge angels? [1 Cor. 6:3]. *Christ's total rule obliterates hierarchy.* The Mediator does not need mediators.[4]

There is a massive difference between distinction and division. While there is no division between God's sons and daughters, there is distinction. For example, Christian unity does not eliminate race, status, and gender. Instead, unity in Christ transcends those distinctions because Christ is so much better, and is what ultimately unifies God's people. Christian unity does not eliminate our distinctions because God, in His providence and creativity, has made us distinct from one another. The same is true with those He "gave . . . to be pastors and teachers" (Eph. 4:11). Pastors are not more holy, more loved, or in better standing with God. They are not divided from the people of God, but they are distinct. The Lord has given them to His Church so they may equip and prepare God's people for ministry. Elton Trueblood stated it well:

> The ministry is for all who are called to share in Christ's life, but the pastorate is for those who possess the peculiar gift of being able to help other men and women to practice any ministry to which they are called.[5]

In some sense, a pastor is to leave the ministry the moment the pastor enters the ministry. The pastor is no longer to "do the ministry," but instead is to "prepare God's people for ministry" to each other and to the world. Of course, in another sense, our identity as Christ-followers means we are always a servant and never above any task. But the role of pastor is divinely designed to prepare others for ministry, not to perform ministry. John Stott, writing on the role of pastors, stated,

> The New Testament concept of the pastor is not of a person who jealously guards all ministry in his own hands, . . . but one who helps and encourages all of God's people to discover, develop, and exercise their gifts. His teaching and training are directed to this end, to enable the people of God to be a servant people. . . . Thus instead of monopolizing all ministry himself, he actually multiplies ministries.[6]

For equipping—a biblical approach to ministry—to occur in a local church, the pastors and the church as a whole must hold tightly to the conviction that all of God's people are ministers. Why don't pastors embrace a conviction to prepare God's people instead of performing ministry? And what stops churches from valuing a ministry that equips people?

Why (Some) Pastors Don't Prepare

Perhaps you have encountered the sound guy who doesn't want anyone else fiddling with the soundboard. Let's call him Ned. At first, you conclude that Ned probably knows best. After all, Ned is able to find *that* buzz, has saved the day multiple times, and uses words you don't understand. You reason that you are an idiot and that you should not concern yourself with things too marvelous for you. But then someone new comes to your church, or an old friend from college visits, and looks at the soundboard, assuming you are able to pick the lock Ned placed on it. You discover that more than one person on the planet understands sound systems, and you begin to sense that perhaps the system has been intentionally designed so no one else can possibly run it.

Ned has built the sound system around himself, for himself. In the same way, some pastors build ministry around themselves, for themselves. And they do so for at least four reasons.

Job security. Just as Ned designed a system where he is necessary, some pastors are hesitant to develop others for ministry because they fear they will become unnecessary to the church. They reason, "If others can do the tasks people think I am paid to do, then what will happen to me?" While the desire of a pastor to provide for his family is understandable and commendable, a Kingdom-minded pastor loves the idea of "working himself out of job." He understands he is an interim pastor, given temporary responsibility for a group of people, and he wants to fulfill his calling—to prepare people for ministry, not to hoard ministry to himself.

In some sense, pastors are absolutely supposed to work themselves out of job. In another sense, if pastors will work themselves out of a job, they will always have one. There will always be a need for godly leaders who are committed to preparing others for ministry.

Insecurity. Just as Ned builds a system that necessitates him, some pastors need to be needed. They love to hear statements like,

"I can't imagine anyone but you praying for me at the hospital," or "We do not know where our church would be without you." Ministry can stroke the ego of an insecure leader who purpose-fully neglects preparing people for ministry because he needs the affirmations of doing ministry.

It takes a secure leader to prepare others for ministry, a leader who realizes he/she is already approved by the Lord, already accepted by Him. And because His approval and acceptance is per-fectly and permanently fixed on the leader, the leader is liberated to prepare and equip others.

Pride. Prideful leaders will always struggle to develop others. Just as Ned thinks no one can run the board like he can, prideful leaders see no need to develop others because they actually believe no one will be able to lead like they lead. We have even heard lead-ers imply that the entire leadership structure of a ministry would need to change if the leader were taken out because "no one is capable of leading the way I lead." A prideful leader typically does not think in terms of development because, after all, the team is there to serve the leader and "the leader's vision." Prideful leaders fail to see themselves as servants of the team with a responsibility to develop others. In these cases the church exists for the pastor rather than the pastor for the church.

Idolatry. Releasing ministry to others is impossible for the leader who holds tightly to ministry as his or her reason for being. Ministry can be an attractive idol because it is rarely called out as sinful. It is an idol that others applaud you for.

Local church ministry can be thrilling, even addictive. Seeing the Lord transform lives and bring people into a relationship with Himself provides a buzz that nothing in this world can provide. And because we are prone to replace God on the throne of our lives with something else, something less, ministry can easily become the god of a church leader. There is a temptation to love ministry more than God, a tendency to rejoice more in the ministry God has given us than in God Himself.

Jesus knew the temptation to commit ministry idolatry would be very real. After He sent out His disciples to minister to people in towns, they returned filled with joy. They were thrilled because they had experienced the great joy of God working through them. "Even the demons submit to us in Your name," they declared (Luke 10:17). Jesus affirmed the authority He had given them but also gave them a caution: "Don't rejoice that the spirits submit to you, but rejoice that your names are written in heaven" (v. 20). In other words, be careful of what ultimately causes you to rejoice.

If we only rejoice in God because of what He is doing through us and not because of what He has already done for us, we cherish our ministry more than Him. If our awe for what He is doing through us surpasses our awe for what He has done for us, we have made ministry our god.

The renowned pastor Martyn Lloyd-Jones battled cancer and poor health in his final months. His biographer, Iain Murray, asked him how he was coping with his shrinking influence, the inability to be used by God to minister to the thousands that he had previously been serving. Martyn Lloyd-Jones responded: "'Don't rejoice that spirits submit to you. Rejoice that your name is written in heaven.' I am perfectly content."[7]

If ministry success is our god, we are likely to take the shortest path to greater and greater "victories," but preparing and developing people is never on the shortest path. If ministry idolatry plagues us, we are hesitant to relinquish the ministry that fuels and drives us. We want to be the one, the man, the hero. We are only perfectly content to equip others if our hearts are filled with awe and wonder that we belong to Jesus.

DISCERNING
MINISTRY IDOLATRY

How can we tell if we are prone to committing ministry idolatry? Here are five questions to consider:

1 How much of my contentment is connected to the tide of my ministry influence?

2 Do my prayers reflect that I am more thankful for the salvation He has provided for me or for the ministry He has given me?

3 If I had to choose, which would I prefer: a closer walk with Jesus or a more "effective ministry"?

4 If my ministry were suddenly taken from me, would I still rejoice that my sins are forgiven?

5 Do I seek God only for His blessing and direction or do I also seek God simply for Him?

We can be perfectly content if we rejoice most in the reality that Jesus has separated our sins from us, as far as the east is from the west.

Why (Some) Churches Don't Value Development

The problem does not rest solely on the pastors of our churches. Our pastors have been developed in our churches and in our institutions. They have been hired by churches with an often unbiblical and unhealthy understanding of local church ministry. Many have learned what they know about ministry leadership from a system that perpetuates an unhealthy dependence on pastors. Churches often insist that pastors "do ministry" rather than "equip people for ministry." So why do some churches perpetuate the typical approach to ministry rather than the biblical approach to ministry? Three reasons stand out:

Ignorance. This is *not* to say that churches are filled with ignorant people, but that many churches are filled with people who are ignorant to the biblical approach to ministry. Smart people can display incredible amounts of ignorance. It does not mean they are ignorant, just ignorant about one thing or another. For example, Eric has proven to be completely ignorant about car repairs, air conditioners, and garage doors—essentially anything involving mechanics. Kevin is ignorant about the wonders of ice cream. In all fairness, he is lactose intolerant.

People are often ignorant to the biblical approach to ministry because in many ways it feels so counterintuitive. "So our church hires pastors *not* to do ministry?" Also, "Let me get this straight. We are going to pay pastors to train us to do *their* jobs?" But His Kingdom often feels very counterintuitive. Such is life in the upside-down Kingdom of God where the last are first, the weak are strong, and the poor in spirit inherit the Kingdom.

Clearly people within our churches need teaching and reminding that they are priests. That as Jesus was crucified, the veil of separation was torn, and we are all able to enter His presence. We don't need a priest to take us to God. We are priests. Ministry retained by the professionals is a deep contradiction of this glorious truth. Martin Luther reminds us, "Let everyone who knows himself to be Christian be assured of this and apply it to himself— we are all priests and there is no difference between us."[8] A church filled with people who insist that the ministry is performed by the pastors is a church filled with people who are failing to fully live out their identity as priests.

Comfort. Eric is the only one in his family who is a pastor. Which means at every family and holiday gathering, he is the one asked to pray before the meal. His family knows he is not the only one in the room who *can* pray, not the only one with the Spirit of God, not the only one whom the Lord hears. But it's just easy to ask the preacher. Eric has been asked for years, and this will likely continue. It is the culture that has been created, and it's just comfortable.

It's easy and comfortable to rely on pastors to "do the ministry," especially if that has been the culture and practice in the church. It is simply what people have observed and known. Thus, in many churches, the cycle continues.

Selfishness. Yes, some resist a culture of equipping because they are selfish. Also lazy and narcissistic. For some, refusing to embrace a biblical approach to ministry is a heart issue, not a head issue—a lack of passion, not a lack of knowledge. They are likely to bemoan that "pastors have easy jobs" and lament "life in the real world." In their minds, they give to the church, and are owed some goods and services in return. Of course, shaming them won't change their hearts. Only the grace and kindness of Jesus can.

The Effect

While many pastors do not emphasize equipping the people in a church for ministry, pastors have often entered church cultures that do not value equipping. In other words, both pastors and churches bear some of the responsibility for the lack of equipping that takes place in many churches. And the effect is that no one wins.

When pastors do for the people in a church what the people should be doing for themselves and each other, everyone loses. The body suffers. People are not discipled and developed for ministry. The local community is not served and impacted as she could be. It is the opposite of the effect beautifully described in Ephesians 4. Look at it once more.

And He personally gave some to be apostles, some prophets, some prophets, some evangelists, some pastors and teachers, for the training of the saints in the work of ministry, to build up the body of Christ, until we all reach *unity* in the faith and in the knowledge of God's Son, growing into a *mature* man with a stature measured by Christ's fullness. (Eph. 4:11–13, emphasis added)

Churches and church leaders are wise to long for both unity and maturity. And the Scripture teaches that as people are developed for ministry, growth occurs in unity and maturity—maturity even measured by Christ's fullness.

The beauty of unity. A church is a community of gifted people, not merely a community of people with a gifted pastor. When people are discipled and developed, a church is more unified. Instead of watching the professionals row the boat, all people are invited and trained to row the boat together. And there is some truth to the cliché: *those who row the boat don't have time to rock it.* In other words, when people are focused on serving one another, unity increases.

When people are taught to sit and watch, murmuring and evaluating increases. Because we long for community, people will unite around something. Without equipping in a church, people are likely to unite on criticism instead of around mission. Of course this is what should be expected from consumers. Church consumers quickly grow disappointed when the religious "goods and services" don't match their tastes or meet their expectations.

Equipping changes a church from a mere consumption center to a gathering of people who serve one another and the world around them. A church focused on developing God's people to serve is a church that knows why she is on the planet, and the people are likely to sense the urgency and significance of the opportunity. When a church is overwhelmed with the immensity of the mission, the small issues of disagreement are less likely to overtake her. There is too much mission to focus on.

Growing into maturity. Our maturing is a lifelong process of being formed more and more into the image of God's Son, and a church with an equipping culture intentionally moves people toward Christlikeness. As people are equipped in the Word, Christ is more fully formed in them. As Christ is proclaimed and people are taught with wisdom, they move toward maturity in Christ (Col. 1:28). As people are challenged and equipped, the false dichotomy between the "spiritual of Sunday" and the "mundane of Monday" is destroyed. They represent Him in their homes, their places of work, and in their neighborhoods. They are salt and light in the spheres of influence the Lord has placed them.

The longer that people attend a church that values equipping, the more they grow uncomfortable with only comfortably attending. When developing people is a visible reality in a church, people are able to see that "this church expects me to grow." They are able to see that their faith should consist of more than "attending church a few Sundays a month." They are able to understand that the Christian faith has deep implications for all of life.

When equipping is a value that permeates the culture of the church, those in the church see the opportunities to pursue maturity, to be developed. As opportunities to be developed are shared with the church body, people are able to move toward Christlikeness within the church.

Preparing Our Girls (and People)

Parenting girls is one of the best experiences either of us could have hoped for. It is also intensely sacred. Over about eighteen years we will help our respective daughters to prepare for life outside our homes. There are so many hurdles, barriers, and dangers implicit in preparing them for life. Inevitably, many days and nights will be spent worrying and wondering if our investment, wisdom, and love are bearing fruit. Still, no matter how hard or dangerous the road gets, there are no shortcuts and there is no way to live our children's lives for them. They will have to honor God with their lives for themselves. Our job is to train them, not do it for them. It's the nature of leading our families.

In the same way, the nature of leading a church is to prepare the people of the congregation to live a life of worship for Jesus. Equipping is the call of every pastor. There is no other job description, no matter what is on file with the personnel committee or board of directors. This should be the understanding of every church member, no matter what ministry model is printed on the posters in the foyer. We are a people ruled by God's Word. He has shown us how His Church is to work according to His power. We cannot improve on the plan of the Master, and we must not try.

Do you really want a church that is growing in unity and toward maturity? Then make your cause, your holy cause, the equipping and preparing of God's people. The epidemic of unhealthy churches is the result of churches and church leaders being woefully under-committed to equipping people for the ministry and the mission of God. Without a deep-seated conviction to develop leaders, without a passion for equipping—a church will not enjoy the beautiful effect of unity and maturity. A conviction for equipping is essential.

As God's people are equipped for ministry to each other, they are also equipped for ministry and leadership outside the body of Christ. As we develop leaders for both the Church and the world, we must develop them to lead as God leads. We must hold conviction for leadership to be rooted in the character of God. To that critical conviction, we now turn.

LEADERSHIP IN THE
IMAGE OF GOD

You have never talked to a mere mortal.
—C. S. LEWIS

Many have declared Jeff Bezos to be one of the *good* leaders in our century. After all, he started Amazon as an entrepreneur and has effectively scaled it into the world's largest retailer. *Harvard Business Review* and others have placed him at the top of their lists, naming him as the best-performing CEO.[1]

But not all have celebrated the environment Bezos has cultivated at Amazon. In August 2015, a *New York Times* article outlining the "bruising workplace" at Amazon went viral. The article read very similarly to the unauthorized biography on Bezos called *The Everything Store.* In both the book and the article, the culture at Amazon is painted as intense and obsessed over their stated values. It is, however, also described as brutal, toxic, and filled with fear and backstabbing.[2]

While one may love being a customer of Amazon, if the article accurately depicts Amazon, many would hate to be an employee. For example, one of the comments left in response to the article came from Dan Kreft, who served Amazon for fifteen years. He commented:

> Amazon is a great place to learn from fantastically skilled and intelligent people. . . . It's a thrilling place to work if you thrive on pressure and love being a part of something huge and powerful. . . . So go ahead, Work Hard, Have Fun, Make History . . . but defenestrate any silly notions that you matter as a person. I wish Jeff Bezos and Company continued success, but I wonder how much more successful they could be if they would only show the same kind of obsessive care about their employees as they do about their customers.[3]

If you read about the culture at Amazon, you are struck with the undeniable power of culture. Value alignment is powerful. Declaring who you are, hiring around those values, and rooting all activity and action in those values create a strong culture. For rabid internal fans of the Amazon culture, their values are a code that drives behavior, keeps mission primary, and spurs action. For some employees at Amazon, they have the values memorized, teach them to their kids, and apply them to all areas of their lives.

Strong cultures can edify or they can destroy. Leaders can bless and serve people or they can hurt and dominate people.

Leadership in the image of God is very different from the culture depicted in the articles about Amazon. The people of God are different. Our values are different. We are about more than financial success, stock prices, and scalability. We are strangers and exiles in this world, members of His upside-down Kingdom, who are commanded to live honorably among people who are far from God (1 Pet. 2:11–12).

We make a grave mistake if we emulate the rigorous culture of Amazon. While our work is for the Lord and requires our enthusiastic passion, we must view work and leadership as a gift and not a god. We must not value productivity over people. We do not have to trade health for effectiveness. We can be both healthy *and* effective.

Leadership, like everything else in creation, can be used for destruction and selfish gain. But leadership, like everything else in creation, can and should be redeemed for God's glory.

If we are to grow our conviction for developing leaders, we need to see clearly the nature of leadership God has given to us. Our conviction for leadership must be rooted in God's design. As we develop leaders, we must lead as God desires and develop leaders who likewise embrace leadership as our King intended it to be. A clear view of leadership in the image of God will impact both our leadership and the leadership of those we develop. Without this conviction, we will be plagued with an insufficient view of leadership, which always leads to either abusive or passive leadership.

Leadership and Creation

Scripture teaches that God created man in His image and according to His likeness. Theologians have long called this glorious reality the *Imago Dei*. A misunderstanding of this incredible truth can lead to sinfully minimizing the value of humans or tragically lifting them to the place of deity. So, before moving forward in building an argument for developing men and women as leaders as a direct implication of this truth, we must define it. Here is one of our favorite definitions from Dr. Peter Gentry:

> Man is the divine image. As servant king and son of God, mankind will mediate God's rule to the creation in the context of a covenant relationship with God on the one hand and the earth on the other.[4]

Dr. Gentry argues that mankind is the image of God, not just the bearer of some attribute labeled "image of God." This is a really profound statement and we believe consistent with the teaching of Scripture. Mankind is the image of God, taking with them the rule and reign of God wherever they go. Not only this, mankind bears the Father's likeness as any natural son or daughter would. There is no doubt our likeness has been marred by the effects of sin, but if you look rightly you can still see reflections of Him in every human. The implication of this view leads us to see mankind's creation with an implicit and incredible destiny. Man was made, as sons and daughters of the High King, to lead His creation to flourish in His care and bask in His glory. We look back to God's original mandate for the leadership He gave people:

> Then God said, "Let Us make man in Our image, according to Our likeness. They will rule the fish of the sea, the birds of the sky, the livestock, all the earth, and the creatures that crawl on the earth." So God created man in His own image; He created him in the image of God; He created them male and female. God blessed them, and God said to them, "Be fruitful, multiply, fill the earth, and subdue it. Rule the fish of the sea, the birds of the sky, and every creature that crawls on the earth." (Gen. 1:26–28)

This decree is absolutely mind-boggling! The matchless, unfathomable God of the universe chose to reveal His glory to the world. And, if this was not enough, He determined to reveal Himself primarily in and through humans. In an unimaginable expression of grace, God has made it so that created man can experience firsthand the majesty and glory of the Uncreated One. God not only created us to bring Him glory and to behold His glory, but He made us to find our fullest joy in savoring His glory.

Still, finding our joy in God and bringing Him glory is not the end of this story.

As we just read, in the garden, Adam is created in the image of God and according to His likeness. Adam is created as the son-king. He is the son of the King and therefore born into the family business of kingdom ruling. Like any prince, Adam is to lead his Father's Kingdom *and* he is to lead it *the way* his Father does. He represents his Father in likeness. Said another way, Adam looks like his Father. His mannerisms, his character, and his nobility all bear his Father's likeness. He is also to rule as his Father's image. Wherever Adam goes, his Father's rule, reign, and laws follow. In light of this royal lineage, God gives him purpose. Adam is commanded to use his leadership as his primary means to perform two actions, for one primary purpose. He is to multiply and subdue, all for the glory of God.

God's people were the first to be given leadership and we were told to reproduce more! We were never meant to be power grabbers, but power givers. As God-appointed leaders, Christians are not just called to have power and authority; we are called to use it to serve others. Being made in His image, our Father gave us an inconceivable mandate. Not only did God make us to thrive within creation, but He also commissioned us to lead this creation so that others in this creation would flourish and thrive.

Theologians in history use the Latin phrase *missio dei* to describe the mission of God. God's plan from the beginning of creation was to entrust leadership to His people so that they might fill the earth with glory-reflecting image bearers who strive to make the earth a glory-yielding garden for the name of Jesus. As part of His mission, we now embrace His command to make disciples of all nations, so that people from every tribe, tongue, and nation will give Him glory (Matt. 28:19). He is creating for Himself a people from all peoples who will be His forever, and we are invited to join Him in His mission.

God's precious first words to His image bearers were given to set in motion this fantastic commission: to lead creation in honoring God and to fill it with more image bearers. We were designed to cultivate, to care for, and to lead creation and creature alike to flourish according to God's design and for God's glory. Mankind was made to lead for the glory of God and the good of others.

Leadership and the Fall

Things went terribly wrong. God had instructed Adam and Eve to not eat from one tree in the garden. Satan came to them, and as he still does, called into question what God has already made clear, "Did God really say?" (Gen. 3:1). Tragically, since the moment the fruit hit the dirt in the garden, everything God made for His glory is now distorted and twisted for evil. All the precious gifts of God are now instruments for suppressing His glory and misrepresenting His nature. God's entrustment of leadership has not escaped this fate. The great tragedy of our leadership is not the lack of leading, but the corruption of its noble purpose.

Now, rather than bless others with leadership, mankind oppresses and uses other men and women for personal benefit. This distortion is so pervasive that people are wholly rejecting leadership, rather than the sin that has distorted it! We should hate sin for what it has done to the noble task of leading. Sadly, rather than hate the distortion of God's plan for leadership, we are all, in our sinfulness, unrelenting in our hatred of any influence that attempts to redirect our stubborn wills. In fact, countless pages have been written about the way the culture is rejecting authority carte blanche. If you have led much in recent years, you may have noticed how questioning and cynical people are of any authority.

Perhaps you, too, struggle with receiving leadership. Do you find yourself naturally suspicious of those who lead you? You are not alone. Many people simply do not want to be led. Like our first parents in the garden, stiff-necked and self-assured, we firmly denounce any attempt by God for others to lead us.

People all over the world are crying out in a symphony of complaints. We see leaders through a lens of mistrust and even disdain.

We heap insults on the "fat cats" on Wall Street, employers, politicians, and sadly, even our pastors. And, in many cases, the insults are rightly earned. Mankind has so distorted the good and godly leadership that God intended that we distrust everyone who holds the mantle. But this is nothing new.

Who can find a good king, a right ruler, or trustworthy father? So many men and women throughout the ages have used authority so poorly. Can we really blame others for mistrust? Every one of us has countless stories about leaders in our lives that were not using their power to cause us to flourish, but rather used us for their own gain.

We have enormous destructive capacity. As representatives of the invisible God, we have the terrible capacity to distort and plunder the glory of God. Since mankind was created as the nobility of God, our rebellion is actually a mutiny within the royal family. This is the most sinister kind of rebellion! Rather than represent the character of God and the glory of His Kingdom, we use our leadership to dominate and destroy others. We use insidious weaponry to dominate rather than cultivate. Created to be trustworthy, noble servant rulers, mankind has used the leadership given to them to promote tyranny and destruction.

This seems really intense, doesn't it? Surely that is not true of you, of us? Many of us sit every day in churches, in homes, and in places of business and don't think we are acting all that destructive. I mean . . . we aren't Hitler or Mussolini, right? But overt evil is not the only way to miss the mark of leadership. Political oppression or domestic domination is not the only way to misrepresent God through leadership.

It's easy to forget that the failure of Adam's leadership in the garden was passivity, not aggression. Adam failed to cultivate the garden. Adam failed to keep the weeds out. The weed of evil crawled into the garden in the form of a serpent.

The crafty Enemy came between Eve and the life-giving promises of God. In that infamous moment, Adam failed to protect Eve and he failed to rebuke the serpent. He did not use his God-given leadership over creation, over serpents, to help Eve flourish according to the Word of God. Eve in the same way submitted to a dust-born creature rather than the Exalted Creator. Rather than embrace her role as God's caretaker, she bowed to the influence of evil in the form of a serpent.

Adam's poor leadership takes but one generation to produce the worst kind of evil. One generation from the rich, life-giving soil of the garden, Adam would find the body of his murdered son buried under bloodstained dirt. His poor leadership led to placing his murdered son in the soil, rather than reaping life-giving fruit from it. This is the produce of bad leadership. This is the fruit of rejecting the call to lead. One generation outside the garden, Cain is destroying the image of God rather than filling the earth with it. He isn't reproducing glory-giving people; he is burying them under dirt and jealousy.

Each one who has been placed in a position of leadership carries with us tremendous responsibility, and so do those we develop for leadership. Should we fail to lead as God has designed, we beckon disaster to enter into our world. Should we develop leaders apart from God's design, we actually help propagate destruction and misery rather than life and hope.

How can we reconcile this current mistrust of leadership and the historic reality that God made men to lead?

Praise be to God, Jesus redeems.

Leadership and Redemption

Jesus is redeeming our leadership for His glory. *What if in and through the Church, God made His people into a different kind of leader?* What if God made Christian men and women into leaders that could be trusted, counted on, and even loved?

Leadership is not bad, but it is very powerful. We all know that powerful things are dangerous and must be handled with extreme caution. There is a reason we don't let kids play with matches. It's not because the matches are bad, but rather it's the known fact that kids often fail to use things wisely. Think about it this way: Leadership is much like nuclear energy. It is able to warm a whole city or bring it to waste in death and destruction; it's all in how it is used.

God created mankind with enormous potential when He made us in His image. In our nobility, we have within us the potential to reflect the indestructible life in God. We are sons and daughters of God; we are His very likeness! When others lay eyes on us, they have the capacity to see something of the invisible God. They can see a picture of what He is like; they can enjoy His majesty and beauty. What if your leadership and the leadership of those you develop could be used to point people to our Creator and King? What if your church embraced the responsibility to develop leaders who lived for the glory of God? God's Church cannot embrace the indiscriminate pragmatism of contemporary leadership practices. A disturbing amount of leadership training being utilized today fails to stop and ask what God wants from our leadership. Even Christian education often promotes effective leadership habits and practices without ever challenging motivation or intent. This approach to development only reproduces a Christian-sprinkled approach to leading, and results in leadership that is self-sufficient and self-serving. Chillingly, our equipping can be all too much like giving murderers better knives.

However, in Jesus Christ, our leadership can be redeemed for His glory. He is full of grace and truth, and as He continually transforms His people, leaders who belong to Him likewise lead with grace and truth. The way our churches train and develop leaders can become as a spring of fresh water spilling out into a dry land. The leaders coming out of our churches, with eyes fixed on the glory of God, can offer the life-giving care, protection, and guidance our world desperately needs.

Leadership and the Glory of God

The primary purpose for our leadership mandate is to make known the glory of God by leading others to flourish in God's design. It's that simple. The goal of all creatures, all gifts, and all leadership is to magnify the matchless glory of God throughout the universe. Paul says it this way: "For from Him and through Him and to Him are all things. To Him be the glory forever. Amen" (Rom. 11:36). We must open our eyes to see that everything God has given to us is fuel to make much of the One who gave it.

Everything we do, every moment we experience, every resource at our disposal is a tool to show the cosmos the greatness of the God who reigns above. In exactly this way, God has given the gift of leadership to Adam. To you. To the people in your church.

God's gift of leadership is not for Adam's sake and it is not for yours. It's for God's sake; it is for His renown. So many times we find ourselves using the platform we have been given to make ourselves more famous, powerful, or wealthy. We use the gifts He gives us to earn more applause, to increase our power, and to gain more wealth. It becomes easy for us to use people to improve our own situation. We use our leadership capacities to get people to do what we want them to do. Many times, the result is more income or more power for us. It is fleshly and natural for us to use our gifts to make much of ourselves. We lead people, and we want people to *know* we led them. Sadly, many don't just want to lead greatly, but also want to be known as great leaders. But this isn't what God intended.

The prophet Habakkuk saw God's destiny for creation. He could see the future reality when God's people, restored unto His image, would spread out all over the world. When this day comes, Habakkuk foresaw a people who use the glory shared with them to make much of God Himself. He saw what God was doing by commanding these image bearers to rule over and fill the earth.

For the earth will be filled with the knowledge of the LORD's glory, as the waters cover the sea. (Hab. 2:14)

Again, God's plan from the beginning of creation was to entrust leadership to men and women so that they might fill the earth with glory-reflecting image bearers who strive to make the earth a glory-yielding garden for the name of Jesus.

To think that the invincible God would use frail men to show the world His glory is staggering. God determined that He would use broken men and women, redeemed by His Son, to become ambassadors to the world. God not only designed to save men and women by grace through faith, but He determined to use men and women to deliver this saving message. He had every method at His disposal for bringing His will to pass. Yet, God chose to use mankind to bring glory to Himself. He designed for men and women to reflect the nature and character of God. He has chosen you and the people in your church.

As you lead and as you develop leaders, you must do so in accordance to His plan. What must leadership look like for the people of God? What must leaders, who embrace leadership in the image of God, do?

What Leaders Must Do

Whether the children in our homes or spiritual children in discipleship, we are called to lead others to flourish. We are leading people to properly reflect the nature of God and to join us in leading others to do the same. The leadership God has entrusted to mankind can be placed into three primary activities:

1. **Leaders are called to *reflect* God's glory.** God-centered leadership is expressed by leaders who embody the character and nature of God in their own lives as much as a pardoned sinner can.
2. **Leaders are called to *replicate*.** God-centered leadership is rightly employed when it aims to fill the whole earth with other renewed image bearers by spreading the gospel and multiplying children of God.
3. **Leaders are called to *cultivate*.** A God-centered leader strives to cultivate an environment where others will flourish in light of the glory of God.

Leaders are called to reflect *God's glory.*

The first calling of every leader is to image God as faithfully and fully as a redeemed sinner can. This is the primary way we reflect the glory of God. When the world sees a Christian leader, it should be a showcase for the spectacular character of the immortal God. We represent His character and nature in our own. His loves, hates, ethics, passions, and purposes are expressed through us. Do not be deceived; God is far more concerned with the leader's personal sanctification than He is with the leader's ability to influence others. How can we confidently say this? It's actually quite simple . . .

God does not *need* your leadership. Don't get us wrong; He *wants* you to lead, and He *wants* you to lead well. But, do not mistake God's desire as dependence on His creation. He is not dependent on us. He is the Lord of heaven and earth and does not need anything, "since He Himself gives everyone life and breath and all things" (Acts 17:25).

When we look at the leaders God has formed throughout the ages, we see over and over again that the Lord cares for their response to His holiness more than how many responsibilities they steward. Do you remember how Moses first handled leadership? While still a prince in Egypt, Moses awakens to the fact that God's people were in need of deliverance. What is his first act of leadership for God's people? Murder, in an outburst of anger, that's what. It would take decades to change the character of Moses. And this change of character was not just steady progress, but a series of steps forward and steps backward. But as we read carefully, God never forsakes forming His servant leader. To the very end, Moses would be called to lead *like* the Lord, not just *for* Him.

Paul, too, while busy planting churches across continents, reminds us that God has not forgotten about his personal sanctification. Paul tells us plainly, "Because of the extraordinary revelations. Therefore, so that I would not exalt myself, a thorn in the flesh was given to me, a messenger of Satan to torment me so I would not exalt myself" (2 Cor. 12:7). Even as Paul spreads the gospel across the world, our heavenly Father is concerned with Paul's humility and character. The story of all of God's leaders, from Abraham to John, and everyone in between, is the story of God relentlessly sanctifying His leaders into His image.

We clearly see God's demand for character in the leaders of the Church through the qualification lists found in the Pastoral Letters. A quick glance reveals the similarity in the lists of qualifications between deacons and elders. The lists are nearly the same. What the lists have in common makes the point: all of God's leaders must have godly character in common because God's leaders reveal God's character through their lives. We would do well, whether leading in the church, home, or marketplace to remind ourselves what God is looking for in His leaders.

An overseer, therefore, must be above reproach, the husband of one wife, self-controlled, sensible, respectable, hospitable, an able teacher, not addicted to wine, not a bully but gentle, not quarrelsome, not greedy—one who manages his own household competently, having his children under control with all dignity. (If anyone does not know how to manage his own household, how will he take care of God's church?) He must not be a new convert, or he might become conceited and fall into the condemnation of the Devil. Furthermore, he must have a good reputation among outsiders, so that he does not fall into disgrace and the Devil's trap. Deacons, likewise, should be worthy of respect, not hypocritical, not drinking a lot of wine, not greedy for money, holding the mystery of the faith with a clear conscience. And they must also be tested first; if they prove blameless, then they can serve as deacons. Wives, too, must be worthy of respect, not slanderers, self-controlled, faithful in everything. Deacons must be husbands of one wife, managing their children and their own households competently. For those who have served well as deacons acquire a good standing for themselves, and great boldness in the faith that is in Christ Jesus. (1 Tim. 3:2–13)

God's demand for godly character doesn't stop with church leaders. Rather, in Jesus, God is working to form all of His people into the image of His Son. As the Son perfectly represents the Father, so God wills and works for us to do the same.

It is not first the work of our hands that pleases the Lord, but the condition of our hearts. We cannot go on leading or living as if our results are God's primary concern. Our leadership results alone do not honor God. We cannot hide behind our accomplishments. The ends do not justify the means in God's Kingdom. We cannot see our leadership as bringing God glory simply by the results our leadership produces. *Why* and *how* we lead is much more important than *what* we lead. As we develop leaders, likewise, we must train them that the *why* and *how* of their leadership is critically important.

God's glory is best revealed through the personal transformation that results from encountering God's glory. If a church is to ever become an epicenter for developing leaders, we cannot overlook this first critical leadership action. Our leaders, unlike any others, must be faithful to reflect the glory of God through their own lives. God's Word makes it clear; the Lord requires leaders who will reflect His nature and His character for His renown.

Leaders are called to replicate.

As leaders who bear God's image, we have been given a profound ministry. We have a cosmic destiny to see Jesus hailed as King across the whole world. God has designed us to accomplish His mission by demonstrating God's Kingdom and declaring the gospel of Christ to the world. We move forward with confidence, knowing that God will extend His Kingdom through us. Through us, God will call others to come to Jesus and be changed. As we lead, God is calling others to be born again and begin the lifelong journey of being conformed to the image of Christ. By His design, we are not called to simply be image bearers, but to replicate other image bearers! We are not called to simply be His disciples, but also to make disciples.

For Adam and Eve, the initial mandate for God's image bearers was to procreate more image bearers. Tragically, Adam and Even ceased to honor God and so every child after them would follow in their rebellion. However, our faithful God would not see His design for mankind thwarted. From the garden to Christ's return, the Scripture reveals the Father's dedication to restore His image in mankind and to set them on a course to reproduce God-honoring image bearers for His glory.

Generations after the Fall, God would recommission mankind by calling another leader to take up the calling to fill the earth with worshippers of the true God. This time, however, God makes it clear that He will not only give the calling, but He will bring it to pass.

> The LORD said to Abram: "Go out from your land, your relatives, and your father's house to the land that I will show you. I will make you into a great nation, I will bless you, I will make your name great, and you will be a blessing. I will bless those who bless you, I will curse those who treat you with contempt, and all the peoples on earth will be blessed through you." (Gen. 12:1–3)

There is no doubt that God is commending the very same leadership to Abram that he did to Adam. Abram is to obey the mandate, to fill the whole world with the knowledge of the glory of God. He is essentially saying, "Abram, I'm going to bless you so much that you and the nations will know that I am the Lord. But, Abram, this blessing is not just for you, but, through you, for all the nations." God has not simply determined to bless His people by revealing His glory. He transforms us by glory. Further still, we not only receive God's glory, we show it and spread it. When God reveals Himself to Abram, He is not just looking for a worshipper. Instead, He is aiming to channel His grace and mercy through and to mankind once again. He is looking for a leader to call others to worship Him, and in doing so, to find eternal joy and life. The Father doesn't just want the worship of one tribe; He wants them all.

In His final words, Jesus brings this call to replicate to bear on His disciples. The Scripture says,

> The 11 disciples traveled to Galilee, to the mountain where Jesus had directed them. When they saw Him, they worshiped, but some doubted. Then Jesus came near and said to them, "All authority has been given to Me in heaven and on earth. Go, therefore, and make disciples of all nations,

baptizing them in the name of the Father and of the Son and of the Holy Spirit, teaching them to observe everything I have commanded you. And remember, I am with you always, to the end of the age." (Matt. 28:16–20)

In His command, Jesus is rearticulating the most ancient command given to man by God. As "they worshipped Him" the disciples are called to go and replicate more disciple worshippers of all nations. This is how God has designed leaders to use their power and influence.

God has designed His people to lead. From the first recordings of history God has made it clear that He has designed creation to be led by His covenant people. More than that, He has determined what His people are to do with the leadership entrusted to them. Whether you are called to lead in the home, the marketplace, the church, or in the city, His people are called to lead others to worship Jesus Christ.

It is not enough for His people to be good citizens of God's Kingdom. We are to be ambassadors of this Kingdom, calling and teaching others to join us in our everlasting allegiance to God through Christ. There is no more noble or truer human leadership than to guide and point others to life in Christ. In fact, every ounce of leadership entrusted to us by God is a stewardship. No matter how much influence we have, we are responsible for what we do with it. Either we are working to replicate worshippers of God, or we risk spending our entrustment multiplying a rebellion against God.

Leaders are called to cultivate.

There is a distinction between Christian leadership and all other leadership in the world. Christian leadership is a vivid picture of God's image in humanity. All other forms of leadership, even the most humanitarian of efforts, are (at best) dim reflections and distorted pictures of the majesty of the invisible God. Christian leadership, on the other hand, is specifically designed for the glory of God and the good of others; there is no other purpose. Christian leadership, like no other kind, with the posture of a servant aims to cultivate the world so others can flourish according to God's design. Jesus tells us plainly what our leadership must look like.

> "But it must not be like that among you. On the contrary, whoever wants to become great among you must be your servant, and whoever wants to be first among you must be a slave to all. For even the Son of Man did not come to be served, but to serve, and to give His life—a ransom for many." (Mark 10:43–45)

In an age where leadership is often used to build self, to build platform, to build job security, to build wealth, and to build power, Christian leadership is about giving one's self away to God's design and destiny for mankind for His glory in Christ alone. In the garden, Adam and Eve are told to cultivate, to care for, God's garden. The sense of this command is that this first family is meant to be a caretaker and an administrator of God's provision and protection to the world around Him. They are to help tend the garden in such a way that it continues to be a place of thriving.

After the fall of humanity, God made it clear that He still desires His people to provide this kind of leadership. He has designed His people to help others to become all that God has destined them to become. We are not simply here to bear fruit, but to create environments where others, inside and outside the family of God, can be fruitful and can experience the peace of God. Of course, the primary motivation for this cultivation is that people in these environments will thrive spiritually. First and foremost, we want men and women to have peace with God through Jesus. However, God has also sent His people into the world to be a common grace to the world that all people may taste the grace of God and the peace of God in this lifetime.

During the exile into Babylon, Israel was to learn this lesson. Surely they wondered how to live in a land that was not their home. Should they protest and picket? Should they isolate themselves? On the cusp of entering the capital city of those who had killed, raped, and enslaved them, God speaks this word to them:

> This is what the LORD of Hosts, the God of Israel, says to all the exiles I deported from Jerusalem to Babylon: "Build houses and live in them. Plant gardens and eat their produce. Take wives and have sons and daughters. Take wives for your sons and give your daughters to men in marriage so that they may bear sons and daughters. Multiply there; do not decrease. Seek the welfare of the city I have deported you to. Pray to the LORD on its behalf, for when it has prosperity, you will prosper." (Jer. 29:4–7)

The word translated *welfare* is transliterated as "shalom." As has been said often by Tim Keller, "shalom" is "the webbing together of God and man with all creation to create universal flourishing and wholeness. In Psalm 102 God has made the world like a garment with billions of entities interwoven to make up the beauty of all that is created. Sin has come in and torn a whole in the fabric." Keller then explains that this "universal flourishing" encompasses all aspects of human life.

For mankind to flourish is for mankind to spiritually flourish, psychologically flourish, sociologically flourish, and physically flourish. When God tells His people to seek the shalom of the city, He is talking about working toward stitching that fabric back together by the power of God. God's design for His people, even in their conquered state, was to be a blessing to those around them. He commanded them to move into the neighborhoods, start businesses, and have children. As God's people, they would strive to live according to the image of God, and in so doing bring light and life to those around them in kindness, justice, and goodness. God's desire was that the very people the Babylonians conquered would be common grace to the Babylonians.

God was commanding these heads of families to take the promised blessing of God, not forgotten in the captivity, and to bring it to bear on the world around them. Even in a land that was not their own, they were blessed so that they might be a blessing, and in so doing, cause the world around them to flourish. This is what the leadership mandate looks like in a fallen world. God's people, whether at work in the marketplace, leading at church, or caring for family, are to cultivate the surrounding soil.

As we develop leaders, we should ask ourselves and teach them to ask themselves whether people thrive or wither under our care. Whatever is in your care, if you are leading according to God's design, should be a place of life and shalom. As thoughtful gardners, God's leaders must make the world around them the place where others grow to their full God-given potential in Christ.

Back to Bezos

The world benefits from godly leadership. Though people may not realize it, they long for the influence of God's people, the cultivated culture that results when God's people live honorably and lead with integrity. People intuitively don't want to dwell for long in cultures of destruction and humiliation.

Though Jeff Bezos is accused of creating a toxic culture at Amazon, in his defense, he confessed that no one would want the culture described in the watershed article. Not him. No one. He said he would not want to work at Amazon if the Amazon depicted in the scathing report was true, which he insists is not the case at all. In his e-mail to employees, responding to the *New York Times* article, he wrote, "Anyone who is working in a culture like the one described in the *Times* would be crazy to stay."[5]

Without God's people leading according to God's design, any culture will inevitably deteriorate. Culture in church, home, and the workplace will self-destruct without God's people distributing His grace through their leadership. We must be leaders and develop leaders who reflect, replicate, and cultivate.

We must lead in the image of God and for the Kingdom of God. Let's look next at leadership for the Kingdom of God.

LEADERSHIP FOR THE
KINGDOM OF GOD

*It is not what a man does that determines whether
his work is sacred or secular, it is why he does it.*
—A. W. TOZER

Both of us have hobbies. Eric likes to play basketball, and Kevin
likes to watch *Star Wars*. With the release of the seventh film,
Kevin rewatched all six episodes *and*, for "their own good," made
his daughters suffer through them too. Surprisingly, all three girls
really like it!

For those born before 1980, the *Star Wars* trilogy was an epic
about a young man learning to wield the power of the force for
good to liberate an oppressed universe from an evil empire. A significant thread in the plot was the hope embraced by the young
Skywalker that his father, Lord Vader (known previously as Anakin
Skywalker), commander of the Empire forces, would see the error
of the dark side of the Force and join the fight against the evil
Emperor.

In May 1999, the *Star Wars* trilogy was expanded by the sub-
sequent release of three more films, all serving as prequels to the
original trilogy. For those like the Peck kids who watched the films
in chronological order, the story makes a different impression. In

the three prequels, among other things, we see the making of Lord Vader. The films follow Anakin Skywalker from innocent childhood, to a good-natured (if not a bit ambitious) young Jedi in training, to his rise as a powerful, evil tool of the dark side.

From this perspective, the story line is especially tragic. They see a young boy, rescued from slavery by a heroic Jedi and trained to become a hero himself. As a young Jedi-in-training, Anakin battles those who have embraced the dark side and witnesses firsthand their evil and treachery. The shocking story line of the prequels follows the young man, with such potential for good, slowly turning to embrace the dark side. His betrayal is so complete, the darkness so embraced, that Anakin Skywalker is unrecognizable by the close of the third film. His hands stained with blood and his heart full of hate, he becomes the evil Lord Vader who willingly vows to serve the evil Emperor.

Why would someone with such promise willingly embrace such a dark destiny? If this fictional story reflects the real human condition, and we think it does, then the answer is troubling. Young Anakin's journey to the dark side is accompanied by an insidious guide. He is seduced by the effective use of leadership skills wielded by an evil leader. Throughout the prequel we learn that the evil Emperor begins as a winsome yet conniving statesman, Senator Palpatine. He skillfully navigates the political scene, posturing humility and promoting well-being for all. He is self-effacing, publically kind, and commands a crowd with inspiring speech. But at the same time we watch helplessly as his compliments, seeds of distrust in authority, and feeding of Skywalker's ego serve to woo the young Jedi's confidence and allegiance. There is no doubt; Senator Palpatine is a talented leader. The scary twist in all this is that once the hook is set, there is no escape for Anakin. In the beginning, Senator Palpatine persuades Skywalker to follow him under the illusion of serving good, but in the end Skywalker will follow headlong into brazen evil. The point that we cannot miss is that while the skill of leadership is a very powerful thing, it is the purpose of leadership that determines the destiny of mankind.

God is intimately concerned with *why, how,* and to *where* we lead people. In the last chapter, we concluded that God has designed the people of God to lead. We were created in His image and His likeness so that we would be fit creatures to rule over God's creation. God intentionally fashioned mankind with leadership in mind. There is no creature like us in all the galaxies in the universe. Yet, we must remember that our leadership comes not from our own determination, but as a gift and stewardship from our Creator. Our leadership comes from our relationship with the Lord. Therefore, our leadership is not for our benefit, but for the glory of the One who entrusted us with it. And this is a delight for us, since we know that our Creator, our God, is also our gracious Father.

Our leadership is primarily expressed as vice-regents of our Father's Kingdom. God's people are to move throughout creation, under the rule of God, leading others to obey the same righteous rule. This rule is no tyrannical reign, but God's perfect Kingdom, in which joy, peace, and righteousness flourish (Rom. 14:17). We are not building homes, churches, communities, and companies in whatever fashion we see fit. Rather, authentic leadership is guiding others according to God's character and for God's purposes. Developing this kind of leader is one of the most crucial duties of the local church. If the local church doesn't develop leaders for the Kingdom of God, who else can?

George Ladd defines the Kingdom of God this way:

The Kingdom of God is His kingship, His rule, His authority. When this is once realized, we can go through the New Testament and find passage after passage where this meaning is evident, where the Kingdom is not a realm or a people but God's reign. Jesus said that we must "receive the kingdom of God" as little children (Mark 10:15 ESV). What is received? The Church? Heaven? What is received is God's rule. In order to enter the future realm of the Kingdom, one must submit himself in perfect trust to God's rule here and now.[1]

The salvation of God's people is not only an issue of forgiving sin and justifying sinners, but also a work of adoption into a royal family and a transfer of citizenship into an eternal Kingdom (Col. 1:13). As the community of the new Kingdom, God's Church must be fully dedicated to developing the people of God to lead as adopted royalty and vice-regents.

The world desperately needs these leaders to guide them out of the darkness! Tragically, the world apart from Christ is not just living independent of God; rather, the lost are presently living under the horrible rule of Satan and sin. Unbelievers are part of a perverse, wicked kingdom. This kingdom of darkness destroys, enslaves, and kills all within its borders. In slavery to sin, our neighbors, family, coworkers, and friends are bowed in servitude in the worst kind of tyranny. As we watch the news, we see horrible testimonies across the globe of life under the rule of this dark kingdom. The hearts of God's people break at the injustice in North Korea, the torn families in Sudan, the proliferated sex trade of Southeast Asia, the countless signs of evil in our own cities, and the list goes on and on. What hope do the nations have for deliverance from the tyranny of this horrific kingdom?

With the coming of King Jesus, there is now, presently, the start of a new and glorious Kingdom, one full of people submitted to the rule of God and receiving all His matchless grace. As those who have born again, and indwelled by the Spirit of God, the people of God have the holy duty and unspeakable delight in helping others to enter into this new Kingdom. The people of God are called to lead others into the light of the Kingdom of God, to help them escape the terror of the darkness. We work to see others reject the dark reign of sin and to come into the joyful Kingdom under the reign of God.

Jesus tells us plainly, the Father has appointed Him Heir and King of the Kingdom (Matt. 28:18). His commission to His people is to go into all the world, into every place, and to teach men and women to submit also to the rule of God by the Spirit of God (Matt. 28:19–20). The glorious reality of this command is the opportunity to invite others into the rule and protection of the kindest, most powerful, most long-suffering King in all the universe. This is the very essence of Christian leadership.

We lead by guiding others into joyful submission to King Jesus. In order for our leadership to be most potent, our leadership must be consistent in word and action. We invite people into this glorious Kingdom by living according to God's Word and by declaring the gospel. When God's people express this kind of leadership together in their community, God's righteous rule shines through the corporate witness of the Church. J. I. Packer says it this way:

> The task of the church is to make the invisible kingdom visible through faithful Christian living and witness-bearing. The gospel of Christ is still the gospel of the kingdom, the good news of righteousness, peace, and joy in the Holy Spirit through entering a disciple's relationship to the living Lord. The church must make its message credible by manifesting the reality of kingdom life.[2]

When we see every believer as part of the mandate to lead others to Christ, we see the crucial task of developing leaders put on display. To be a part of a local church is to be a part of a leadership community. God's Church is leading the world out of the kingdom of darkness and into the mercy and grace of the Kingdom of God.

Not only are church leaders called to be leaders themselves for the Kingdom, but the church must equip others to lead. If members of the body of Christ are to be faithful to this Great Commission, they must be developed to lead. Everyone called to be a disciple of Jesus is also called to make disciples of Jesus. There is no doubt that the Spirit of God can use anyone. He does not require great leaders to make faithful disciples, nor does He need great evangelists to deliver the gospel. Nonetheless, the aim of the church is to enable every member to lead others into the Kingdom, so we must work hard to train them for the task.

Sadly, we don't always lead our churches this way. Often the local church is built to make great followers but not great leaders. We often like our congregants to be compliant, but the Kingdom needs more mavericks. We aren't looking for rebels—we have plenty of those—but we do need more mavericks. The local church was built to follow Jesus, the very picture of radical risk-taking to rescue and redeem people. In following Jesus, and helping others be conformed to His image, we are training others to lead against the grain of the present world order.

The Church is to model and preach this new glorious Kingdom of God, not just for those who would walk through our doors, but by developing others to take the Kingdom to every door they walk through. As the Church develops leaders who lead for the sake of the Kingdom of God, these leaders will be used by God to extend the Kingdom of God across the globe. The Kingdom of God has one door—Jesus—but the message of King Jesus is carried to a million places, into every sphere of life, on the lips and in the lives of every equipped disciple.

In Every Sphere of Life

The Church aims to see Jesus rule over every heart. We believe that only in joyful submission to the rule of Jesus can any human truly thrive. One of the primary instruments in this endeavor is for the Church to train and equip leaders to advance the cause of Christ wherever God takes them.

As church leaders we rightly think often about sending gospel leaders into unreached people groups. We work hard to train leaders to go into the most difficult places in the world. We also direct attention, as we should, to developing leaders to serve in our churches. We must develop leaders for the nations and leaders for our churches, but we also must equip God's people to lead in the environments He has currently placed them.

Jesus is the Lord of the Church, but He is also Lord of heaven and earth. He is sovereign, not only over every human kingdom, but also over every domain within every human society. If we want to see the rule of God pervade every society, we must work to train leaders of all kinds within society. Kingdom advancement requires a saturation of Kingdom leaders both across societal borders and across domains within them.

Charles Spurgeon put it this way: "Every Christian is either a missionary or an imposter." The charge to our churches is to prepare the saints to be missionaries to this world, even as God calls some of them to lead in the world. While not every believer will lead in society, the Church must develop the ones God is calling to lead. Just as our churches flourish under great leadership, other organizations and communities are designed to flourish under godly leadership.

The power of God is unstoppable. God has the capacity and desire to work on behalf of His people in all situations. Even in times of calamity or difficulty, there is a unique kind of flourishing available for those under the reign of God. God extends this grace to His people and to those under their care. As godly leaders reflect God's character and purposes in their spheres of influence, even profound difficulties can be redeemed for the glory of God. When unbelievers witness God's people leading with confidence, joy, and grace through adversity, they become captivated by the hope of God's Kingdom. Unbelievers will see the strength of our God over the powers of this decaying present kingdom. They will see our citizens thrive under adversity, and they will long to be a part of the unconquerable Kingdom of Jesus. In this way, even the worst situations enable God's people to lead for God's glory and the good of men and women in their care.

Leaders, trained to lead like King Jesus, have the capacity to point men and women to the ever-present hope being conformed and promises of our eternal God. It is only these leaders, conformed to the image of God, who have the incredible capacity to connect ordinary people to the extraordinary power of God through the gospel.

For those who follow godly leaders, there is constant access to witness the power of living in the Kingdom. True leadership in this world always includes a consistent invitation to be a part of the greatest Kingdom in the universe. Who else but Christ-following Christians, have the good news that powerless sinners can be saved from sin, death, and Satan? Who else has a message that can deliver people from the futility of the gods of money, sex, power, and independence? Leaders who lead according to the rule of this present age can only wield the power of the false gods of this age. But those born of the Spirit have the opportunity, no matter what capacity or venue, to introduce those in our care to the power of God.

As God's image-bearing leaders live according to the promises and character of God and foster environments inviting others to do the same, we will see the Kingdom of God expand. God's plan for expanding His Kingdom through the conversion of men and women must happen in a multitude of organizations and groups of people. As we lead and develop leaders for all spheres of life, God is saving people through the witness and leadership of His people. God is building His Church through everyday lives in everyday situations.

The Church of God must train all kinds of leaders. Not many men and women will lead in the Church, but scores will lead in other spheres. If we do not equip God's people to lead according to God's design inside and outside the Church, they will be left to lead according to the world's design. As we said before, God's design for leadership is not only different in means, it is profoundly different in ends. The world is naturally training God's people to lead in a sinful manner and for sinful results. Inside and outside the Church, we must equip our leaders to lead as God has designed mankind to lead. If we do not give men and women a vision and tools for leading for God's Kingdom, why should we be surprised if they lead for the outcomes desired by the world?

John Stott said, "We should not ask, 'What is wrong with the world?' for that diagnosis has already been given. Rather, we should ask, 'What has happened to salt and light?'"[3] We, and the people we serve, are called by God to be salt and light in the world. Salt and light are in our churches every week; we must equip them to live as salt and light in their places of residence, work, play, and commerce.

Whether in the church or in everyday society, God's people often fail to lead according to God's design. Many continue to lead for their personal ambitions rather than for the Kingdom of God. Sadly, the world has taken notice. But why is this happening? There is no doubt that the ever-present temptation of sin is a major culprit. But what if our lack of training for leaders takes some of the blame? As God calls men and women to lead in churches, business, governments, and in community services, we must take seriously our call to equip them.

What if God's people learned to lead for God's Kingdom rather than for the trophies of personal success? Can you imagine if God's people led churches, companies, government, and community service all over your city the same way God leads His Kingdom? What an incredible difference it would make if believing pastors, doctors, educators, politicians, teachers, and government workers led with Christ's Kingdom in mind. What if we didn't wait for our people to go to university or even seminary to learn to lead, but instead they learned to lead in God's Church?

God's Church has a unique role in training leaders. According to Scripture, the Church stands apart from all organizations in creation as the dwelling place of the Spirit of God. This fact has great importance in our discussion of developing leaders. For, above all other requirements for Christian leadership, one attribute stands apart from the rest: Men and women that lead in God's Kingdom must be controlled by the Holy Spirit of God. This is the difference between Christian leadership and all others forms. Without the work of the Holy Spirit, leadership is bound to remain carnal, lifeless, and powerless. But as we follow the Spirit of God, we are able to lead men and women to encounter the living God. Our perfect example, Jesus, led in fullness of the Spirit (Acts 10:38), and we must as well. When we lead for the advancement of His Kingdom, we must do so in the power of the Spirit.

As we train leaders in the local church, we must insist that leading without the Holy Spirit can never be leadership for the Kingdom of God. Without the regenerating work of God's Spirit, a person will still be mastered by sin and bent toward rebellion. Whether self-delusion or intentional pretense, without God's Spirit human leadership will inevitably lead to destruction for both leader and follower. Leadership that points to anything other than God for life and hope is by definition idolatry. Without God's Kingdom as our aim, the most skillful leadership is still, at best, a lifeless perversion of God's design. No matter where the people of God lead, the Church must equip them to lead for the Kingdom of God by the Spirit of God.

Leading in the Public Square

The "public square" was historically the space in the middle of the city where the community came together. It was here that issues were raised and problems were solved. It was in the public square where business needs intersected government issues and government workers were made aware of the needs of the people. In the public square, society was shaped and the community was fashioned.

Throughout the ages, the public square has changed in form, but not in function. Today, many cities do not have a physical "square" in the middle of the city, but societies still find a way to communicate and convene. The members of our churches spend much of their time in the public square through their work and through community involvement. Those who lead in business, community services, and government represent the voices of our modern public squares. As we train the societal leaders in our congregations to lead for the Kingdom, people in our societies can flourish in ways they never imagined.

Most people spend the vast majority of their waking lives at work. Yet, many churches spend a sparse amount of their exegetical labors helping people apply God's Word to life and leadership in the public square. We must develop leaders for the Church, but we cannot neglect equipping saints to perform the role of leader in society. Abraham Kuyper, a Dutch theologian and former prime minister, said, "There is not a square inch in the whole domain of our human existence over which Christ, who is Sovereign over all, does not cry, Mine!" In other words, a Christian's opportunity to serve God as a leader is not limited to inside a local church. A Christian approach to leadership reaches into every sphere of life, because every sphere of life belongs to God. So our churches must apply Scripture to leading in every sphere, because God sends us there every week. Men and women who have been given the opportunity to lead in business, government, and community services have the ability to advance the Kingdom through their leadership. The Church has the opportunity and the duty to develop the very best gospel-driven leaders in society.

The Church of God alone can unlock the potential of biblically informed skills and bring secular ones under the lordship of Jesus. There is no doubt that universities and programs offer top-notch business skills and excellent leadership training, and church-trained leaders should not have less acumen. Instead, if our churches can step up to the task, Christ-following leaders will be counted among the greatest leaders in the public square. We do not want to reinvent all leadership training, but we must reinterpret it through a Kingdom worldview.

To equip Christians as great societal leaders who impact the Kingdom of God, we must equip and encourage leaders to be both:

1. Stewards and Managers: Societal leaders should steward His resources through skillful management.
2. Culture Makers: Societal leaders should create environments conducive to gospel advancement.

Leaders in Society as Stewards and Managers

There are significant ways that societal leaders can reveal the characteristics of God to the world. Some of God's attributes and character are *best* displayed through management activity. For example, business and government leaders are some of the world's most significant stewards of resources. This kind of leadership displays the wonder of God in a unique way. Throughout the Scripture, God reveals Himself as a kind, providing, caretaking Manager over His creation. Everything, all wealth and honor, is His, and He is the ruler of all things (1 Chron. 29:11–12). He has everything, yet He cares for the lilies of the field (Matt. 6:28). He manages to the detail of the lilies in the field!

As God provides for, guides, and protects all that He owns, societal leaders who manage well have an incredible opportunity to display the wonderful reign of our Great King and Creator God. Each domain has the profound opportunity to see God's character reflected through the skillful management of people.

As *business leaders* are equipped to see their leadership as a means to care for others made in the image of God, a profound mystery is revealed. In an age where employers are known for using and leveraging "human resources," what a wondrous reality that the God of the universe does not leverage us, but instead has designed us to be objects of His mercy and grace. Can you imagine what people would think if they could work in a business where their Christ-centered employer lovingly and selflessly provides for, protects, and guides the employees of the company? A business leader that leads to provide for others rather than exploit others for personal gain honors God in ways others cannot.

Moreover, business leaders, like no one else, are responsible for utilizing the assets to produce goods and services and to accomplish the mission of the company. This is really significant. By managing resources here and now, business leaders can reflect the wisdom of the God who owns all things, for all time. One of the most profound aspects of the leadership mandate in Genesis is the capacity and duty of mankind to reflect the control and management exerted by the Sovereign King over creation.

When God speaks to man in the garden, He commands them to "be fruitful and multiply and fill the earth and *subdue* it and have *dominion* over the fish of the sea and over the birds of the heavens and over every living thing that moves on the earth" (Gen. 1:28 ESV, emphasis added). Wayne Grudem states, "The word translated 'subdue' implies that Adam and Eve should make the resources of the earth useful for their own benefit."[4] As business leaders engage in promoting business activity, they have the potential to glorify God through taking the gifts of creation and turning them into something that provides for the needs of mankind. Business is not a necessary evil. Business, done according to God's law, honors the purpose of God for mankind.

Our hope must be to help God's people dispersed through all society not merely to *tolerate* business, but to view it as a sacred opportunity to reflect the character of God.

Government leaders also have an opportunity to make much of God's Kingdom by displaying God's character through management. The world would pay attention to those who make decisions in light of human flourishing rather than personal advancement and party agendas. Our societies need men and women in our government to be bastions of integrity and fountains of wisdom and care. Citizens long to see government leaders use resources with honesty and selflessness. Of course society does not agree on *how* to allocate resources for the common good, so the matter is complicated. Nonetheless, God is honored when noble and wise care is displayed by those He calls to lead society.

In the United States we are in a crisis of leadership. While the problems of the world continue to press in on our society, there is a growing distrust of leaders. The solution to many of our problems rests with our leadership, but our people often no longer trust those who have authority. One massive opportunity is the capacity to restore this trust. Sebastian Traeger has thoughtfully written:

> When we use this authority wisely and respect the authority God has over us, we show the world around us that authority is designed to be a good thing. This is a truth that is generally not understood or respected in our contemporary culture. Most people think of authority as an evil thing, or at best as something we tolerate to maintain the social order.[5]

A right use of authority by believing leaders of society can bring much healing to the mess we've made out of our communities today. Redeeming leadership goes beyond using authority rightly. Leaders today will have to establish a pattern of using power for the right things as well. Lip service is not enough. The leaders of society cannot just treat people correctly as they lead them; leaders must lead them to right places.

Our Divine King not only rules us rightly, He leads us to places where we will flourish and find life. Therefore, as the believing leaders of our communities are renewed in His image, they can rightly reflect God's Kingdom. These leaders must be developed in our churches to lead as God's ordained leaders for the good of God's creation. As God's representatives, we cannot afford to send our leaders into the risky position of authority without training them to use it biblically. All too often government officials sit in our church services, Sunday after Sunday, but are never equipped to lead according to God's design.

Community service leaders, too at the fundamental level, are in professions of creation care. Education, health providers, environmental work, and other such professions directly demonstrate the care God has for creation. Yet, because of sin, even these wonderful avenues for work are corrupted by greed, apathy, and malice. There is something in each of us that longs for these services to be provided, not just as a way to earn a paycheck, but as a true expression of love and kindness. It is almost startling to the human soul when someone truly demonstrates the character of God through selfless service to the community. A great teacher in a school or a skillful nurse or doctor provide care every day that often feels more like the love of a parent and less like the duty of someone just doing the job for the day.

This kind of "light" causes our eyes, if even for a moment, to look heavenward, reaching for the deeply buried sense that our Creator God is a good Father. Believers who are leading in the community services world can manage their organizations to this reality. As leaders in society are equipped to lead for the Kingdom, the world can be pointed to God. Standing in the public square, our church members can lead others by reflecting our good Creator King through Spirit-empowered provision, protection, and care.

Just as God's Kingdom is manifested in a home through believing parents, so also God's reign can be shown in society through believing leaders whose shining light can cause others to glorify our Father in heaven (Matt. 5:16).

Leaders in Society as Culture Makers

It would not take much effort to convince the average person that the leaders in our society shape our culture. Business activity, with speed like never before, has the capacity to radically shift the tide of culture. We feel the effects of the cultural leaders all around us. We can testify that commercial leadership "reaches out to sell more than a service or product; it sells a way of understanding the world."[6] But, the tide doesn't stop with the business sector. Government policies, school curriculum, healthcare practices, and a litany of other organizations have shaped much of society's culture. From the launch of new technology to Supreme Court decisions, the influence of societal leaders is obvious and far-reaching.

There is a deep hope in the impact societal leaders have on culture. The leaders of society who have new life in Jesus have no less opportunity to shape the culture around them. While history is certainly not moving toward utopia on earth before the return of Jesus, the people of God still have the power to shape the world around them. We cannot remain passive waiting on Judgment Day. God is calling His people to engage in pushing back the darkness in our societies. Born-again societal leaders have a profound stewardship and opportunity to use their influence to challenge sinful paradigms and godless worldviews. Using their influence wisely, Christian leaders can cultivate environments where a biblical worldview can flourish around them. Christian leaders providing an alternative voice to the roar of culture is a common grace to mankind.

In every age the people of God have faithfully been the heralds of God's truth to the world around them. This generation has no less a calling. The leaders of business, government, and community services who worship with us every Sunday have a challenging but crucial task in this moment in redemptive history. Our leaders, engaged in the public square, must be equipped in the great task "to express the gospel message to a new culture in a way that avoids making the message unnecessarily alien to that culture, yet without removing or obscuring the scandal and offense of biblical truth."[7] While not every societal leader will have the same reach to determine culture throughout the city or country, each leader can have a significant impact on the culture within his or her own organization.

Leaders shape the culture of the organization they lead more than any other external force. This organizational culture informs its employees and customers on how the world works, how people should act toward one another, and what the organization exists to do. Through shaping these values, biblically trained leaders can make their organization a place where the gospel seems consistent with the current paradigm or completely foreign. What a profound responsibility!

Employers under the kingship of Jesus serve, not only as managers, but as servant "kings" as well. Employers can have similar influence as parents in a family. Christian parents attempt to create a family culture that highlights, embodies, and exemplifies the gospel message. Parents do this so that their children hear the gospel message and their experiences in the home point to the truth and power of the message. Leaders, in the same way, even in a business, have the profound opportunity to nurture a worldview consistent with the Scripture. Business leaders can establish behavior patterns through their leadership that displays forgiveness, sacrificial leadership, and compassion. And these qualities will serve as launching points for gospel conversations. The hallways of the office can be a highway for grace, humility, and kindness.

Church leaders have been well aware of their responsibility to shape the culture of the church to be consistent with the gospel message. However, we are arguing that this is not enough. We don't want the church to be alone in maintaining a gospel-nurturing culture; culture may be shaped wherever God's people lead. God's Church must make it a critical priority to train leaders to create and shape cultures where people flourish and the gospel is advanced. We must help leaders within our church see their potential to shape their spheres of influence for others to be served and blessed according to God's design.

Leading in the Local Church

While leading in society is one key aspect of cooperation with God's Kingdom advancement in the world, the local church is God's primary means of accomplishing His mission. This statement cannot be overemphasized. While there have been terrible instances of abuse, distortion, and even malicious masquerading the Church remains God's people for God's glory. For all of the failures of the Church, particularly among her leaders, the Church is beautiful.

The Church is not a Christian club, weekly group counseling session, or weekend pick-me-up. Your local church is the beautiful bride of King Jesus! He is jealous for her. He died for her. And He wants her brought home in purity and splendor. This is nothing we can take lightly. The weightiness of these realities should shake us to the core. We should be provoked to think deeply about the purity of our churches and the faithfulness of our leaders. These awesome realities must drive us to a deep conviction for developing the next generation of church leaders. There is nothing more foolish or careless than to trust what is most precious into the hands of the unprepared. As we equip and encourage leaders for God's Church, we must develop leaders who are:

- Models of Character
- Guardians of Doctrine
- Shepherds of Care
- Champions for Mission

Models of Character. Foremost in a leader's development, in any venue, is the stringent testing of his or her character. Leadership for the Kingdom of God requires leaders who live like sons and daughters of the King. This is even more critical in leading in a church than leading anywhere else. The Scripture defines the church's leaders not chiefly in terms of skill but rather in terms of quality of character (1 Tim. 3:1–15; Titus 1:6–9).

As we train and assess leaders for service in our churches we must not assume character. Countless church governing boards and leadership teams are filled with men and women of excellent skill, significant influence, but untested character. If we are not deeply convicted that the wisdom of the Scripture must be obeyed in this regard, we are not building a church for the Kingdom. We are building a social club for our own interests and our own agendas. Without superlative character across the leadership teams of the local church, we can expect the opposition of God, "who opposes the proud" (James 4:6 ESV). That's just plain scary.

Our churches are suffering, as are our leaders. While the following statistics don't offer commentary as to why leaders are challenged in their character, they do provide a context for the necessary conviction for character.

- Thirty-eight percent of pastors said they were divorced or currently in a divorce process.
- Thirty percent said they had either been in an ongoing affair or a one-time sexual encounter with a parishioner.
- Fifteen hundred pastors leave the ministry each month due to moral failure, spiritual burnout, or contention in their churches.[8]

Being a model of character does not mean being a person of perfect character. Rather, modeling character means living a life of significant victory and regular repentance with regard to sin. Leaders in the Church are not sinless; there is only one sinless Leader in the Church! Still, the reputation of every church leader must be above reproach. When we develop future leaders, we must be confident in God's providence. If God calls a man or woman to lead in His Church, then He will supply the grace to walk in a manner worthy of the calling.

Guardians of Doctrine. A local church will not be led for the Kingdom of God unless her leaders are consumed by a passion for the Word of God. The leaders of God's Church are men and women submitted to God's Word and lovers of God's Word. We have no more precious entrustment than the doctrines of God. Without the Word of God, we have nothing to offer those who follow. Leaders who do not see themselves as people of the Book will falsely offer life in their own opinions and practices.

As we look to equip saints to lead in the local church, we cannot overemphasize the need to ensure that they are able to protect and teach sound doctrine. For years this task has been largely entrusted to seminaries and other educational institutions. There is no doubt that these schools have been a great blessing to the Church in fighting for the preservation of healthy doctrine in the Church. Still, there seems to be a disconnect when applying the same standard of doctrinal integrity to leaders not "on the church payroll."

Those who will go into paid ministry leadership positions are often expected to get a quality theological education. However, in many cases, we don't expect leaders who are "just volunteers" to obtain the same level of understanding in the Scriptures. This is an incredible problem. There will always be a spectrum in "ability to teach," but the requirement for leadership in the church (especially that of "elder" or "pastor") is not contingent on the source of a person's income.

Every leader we entrust with a title is also entrusted with the health of the church. When we call someone a leader in the church, we are calling the church to trust his or her words. Recognizing that there are varying degrees of knowledge between leaders, we must still take seriously the call to train our leaders in sound doctrine. What good is it to collect masses of people if our leaders have nothing but empty, powerless words to offer? The gospel of Jesus is what is at stake here (Rom. 1:16; 10:17; John 17:17; Titus 1:9; 2 Tim. 2:15). Paul paints a terrifying future to the Ephesian elders before his departure:

> Be on guard for yourselves and for all the flock that the Holy Spirit has appointed you to as overseers, to shepherd the church of God, which He purchased with His own blood. I know that after my departure savage wolves will come in among you, not sparing the flock. And men will rise up from your own number with deviant doctrines to lure the disciples into following them. (Acts 20:28–30)

One of the primary roles of church leaders, unpaid like Paul, and paid alike, is to protect the sheep of God from those who would destroy them through distorting the Word of God. Do you believe that wolves still prowl in your flock today? If so, we must develop the kinds of leaders who are ready to ferociously guard the flock with sound doctrine. We need our leaders to be able to say along with Paul, "A person should consider us in this way: as servants of Christ and managers of God's mysteries" (1 Cor. 4:1).

Shepherds of Care. "Desiring to excel is not a sin. It is motivation that determines ambition's character. Our Lord never taught against the urge to high achievement, but He did expose and condemn unworthy motivation."[9] Godly ambition is a good thing. We want leaders in our church who *want* to lead God's Church. We are training men and women to have a passionate desire and accompanying skills to make much of Jesus through excellent leadership. Still, we must be careful. There is so much temptation amidst all the leadership books pushed into our hands to produce excellent, but wrongly motivated, leaders for the Church.

There is an ugly secret among paid ministers: leading God's Church can be an opiate for the ego or sedative for a life of ease. The priests of the Dark Ages are not the only clergy to find perks in the power of the pulpit. Ego, respect, comfort, and even money can be motivators for a life in ministry. Paid ministers are not the only ones who find sinful ways to plunder God's Church. The troubling reality is that there are far too many reasons to lead in God's Church that have nothing to do with the Kingdom of God.

Therefore, when we develop leaders of God's Church, we are looking for the right motivations, not just the right profiles. Among all the metaphors God could have used, He chose "shepherd" to describe Himself as a leader and to describe the leaders of His Church. When training leaders for the Church, we must seek to produce shepherds, not just executives. We need to be forming men and women into loving caretakers of the flock, not just effective directors. In one of the most scathing indictments of the leaders of God's people, God says through Jeremiah,

> "Woe to the shepherds who destroy and scatter the sheep of My pasture!" This is the Lord's declaration. "Therefore, this is what the Lord, the God of Israel, says about the shepherds who shepherd My people: You have scattered My flock, banished them, and have not attended to them. I will attend to you because of your evil acts"—this is the Lord's declaration. "I will gather the remnant of My flock from all the lands where I have banished them, and I will return them to their grazing land. They will become fruitful and numerous. I will raise up shepherds over them who will shepherd them. They will no longer be afraid or dismayed,

nor will any be missing." This is the LORD's declaration. (Jer. 23:1–4)

As we train leaders for the Church and for the Kingdom, we must be looking for and developing loving shepherds, not cattle-driving ranchers. The commitment is so great that effective shepherding often comes at great personal cost for the leaders.[10]

Champions for Mission. Every leader in a local church needs to be a champion for mission. We will never build churches that live with abandon for the Kingdom of God without leaders who are tethered to God's desire to save for Himself a people for His own possession. Every leader in the Church must be a follower of Jesus. We are not using this term as a placeholder for being a Christian. Rather, the requirement for being a "follower of Christ" is meant to emphasize that we are actually following Christ! But, where is Christ "going"? Jesus isn't merely going to our living rooms and potlucks. No—*the Son of Man has come to seek and to save that which was lost*! If we want to follow Jesus, He is on the move. He is on a mission to the lost.

If the leaders of God's Church are content to only enjoy the Kingdom, rather than build it, the Church will likely follow them to apathy. God's missionary Church needs missionary leaders. When Jesus was cut, He bled for all nations. When our leaders bleed, they too must bleed a heart for the mission. The scope of the mission of the Church represents the value the Church places on Christ's blood. The Scripture says His blood was the purchase price for people from every tribe and language and people and nation (Rev. 5:9–10). The leaders of God's Church must believe and live knowing He will get all that He paid for.

Don't Create Another Anakin

A Christian leader is not only the man who faithfully preaches every Sunday. Neither is she only the entrepreneur that gives 10 percent of annual profit to Christian causes. The Christian leader is he or she who is indwelled by the Holy Spirit and is obedient to God's leadership to embody His calling on their life in *every sphere of life they find themselves*. While God is working through His Church, He desires to send your church into the world on a mission. His design is to use His people to lead in this world to share His character and demonstrate His righteous rule with the world. Christian leadership is one of God's most gracious gifts to all people, inside and outside the local church.

Anakin Skywalker lost his soul in pursuit of great power apart from a righteous purpose. The irony of this silly illustration is that while millions of *Star Wars* watchers will see the folly of Skywalker, most will embrace it themselves. The power of leadership is intoxicating. The temptation to use it for selfish gain pulls on humanity like gravity. Only the Spirit of God in His people can break the selfishness. The Church has been uniquely designed to develop the leaders God intended for His glory and the good of mankind. God's people, equipped by His Church, can unleash the full potential of leadership by leading in the image of God for the Kingdom of God. For your church to be a leadership locus—to continually develop and deploy leaders—you first must be deeply convinced and convicted of this reality. If you are, let's move on to *culture*.

Culture

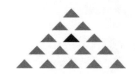

"Developing leaders moves from a deeply held conviction to the very core identity of the Church."

THEOLOGY OF CULTURE

Culture eats strategy for breakfast.
—PETER DRUCKER

"Summit Church, you are sent, instead of dismissed. Sent."

This is how our friend Pastor J. D. Greear closes a worship service. This benediction captures so much of what it means to be a part of The Summit Church in Raleigh, North Carolina. The church leadership speaks weekly to the congregations about living as men and women sent by God "to love God, love each other, and love our world." For The Summit Church, these are not just words; they have become a mantra to a culture. Flowing from conviction, God has established a *culture* for developing leaders who advance the Kingdom of God.

For the newcomer, it takes no longer than a few weeks to figure out what the church wants for its members. The language of "sent" is so common, the opportunities for development and the invitations to engage so pervasive, that it is nearly impossible to escape the cultural pull to join in God's mission. The vision for being equipped and sent for mission is so pronounced and prominent that the members now passionately speak of the vision as their own. Story after story is told of men and women developed within the church and then sent into the world on mission for

God. Campaigns, sermons, and programs are not driving behavior anymore; convictions have seeped into the collective worldview of church. Many would find it unthinkable to have a vision to plant one thousand churches in one generation. For The Summit Church, the goal is not just possible, it's probable.

What power there is when the conviction to develop leaders becomes part of the culture of a church! The playing field is radically changed when everyday people begin to think that being developed to lead God's mission is the normal life for God's people.

Theology and Church Culture

Unhealthy church culture is ultimately a theological problem. Eventually, people behave consistently with their most fundamental beliefs. What the church community believes about God, themselves, and the world will drive the way they interact with each. As we work toward becoming churches that embrace the call to develop leaders according to God's design, we must look carefully at our culture and the underlying beliefs that form it. Culture is too powerful to only get a casual glance.

In looking at church culture, we need to be deliberate and precise. It is all too easy to look at culture as a nebulous concept that attempts to describe the "vibe" of a church. We often jump over a true investigation into church culture and settle for cutting and pasting language from other "successful churches" with hopes to get their results. Instead, we want this chapter to help you understand the beliefs beneath the surface that form church culture so that you can evaluate your culture's beliefs and shape them for the glory of God and the development of His people.

We must get underneath the visible layer of culture, beneath even the *stated* beliefs of culture, and go all the way to the invisible assumptions held by the church. This isn't an easy task, but it is one that must be taken by those who care for the church they serve. The Church needs leaders who build a culture of leadership development from a foundation of precise theological convictions. God's leaders must know what the sheep truly believe and help align these beliefs with the Word of God.

Church culture is formed through the actual beliefs and resulting expressions for a local church about creation, the identity of the local church, and how the local church interacts in the world. Within each of these categories, several basic beliefs build out the church's basic worldview. The following framework synthesizes some of the best thinking on organizational culture and adapts it for use in the local church.[1] The framework is designed to be a tool to build a church culture consistent with developing leaders.

As in pouring a foundation for a house, building culture requires skill and precision. A foundation with cracks and blemishes cannot hold the house; neither can a culture with inconsistent beliefs sustain a leadership development effort. As this chapter moves through the framework, realize that every component of culture contributes to the integrity of the whole foundation. In building the foundation, it is important to see both the belief and the resulting expression of that belief in the following three categories:

1. **The Realities of Creation:** core beliefs that provide the basis for understanding the creation we exist in. From these we form a worldview on how truth is known, how time works, how space affects us, and the essence of humanity.
2. **The Household of God:** a set of beliefs that form a paradigm for understanding the identity of the local church. These beliefs tell us who we are as the local church, how we interact with each other, and what it means to belong to the church. All the beliefs and assumptions in this category add up to a worldview about how the members of a church think about themselves and interact with each other. The local church is portrayed in Scripture as the household of God[2]—thus the most appropriate way to think about the

interaction of church members is that of members of God's household, coheirs of His inheritance, and brothers and sisters under the care of God the Father.

3. **The Mission of God:** a set of beliefs that provides an understanding as to why the Church exists, how it relates to the non-Church world, and what the Church is meant to accomplish. As the "sent" people of God, the Church is the instrument of His mission (John 20:21).[3]

The Realities of Creation

In order for a church to ever become a leader-producing church, there are several foundational beliefs about the realities of creation that a church must hold. Beliefs about *truth, time and space, and the nature of humans* all greatly impact the cultures leaders cultivate.

Trust in God's Word (truth): There is so much confusion in the world about the nature of truth and how we come to know it. The epistemology (ways of knowing truth) of our generation today is a tragic mash-up between popular culture and historic Christian thought. What is left in our society and, by extension, our churches is a view of truth that is at best inconsistent and at worst incoherent. We don't say this to disparage the culture in which we are living, but to underline the fact that our people breathe this air. Our members and their children live in a world that, at its very core, is confused about how we even come to know what truth is. This is a significant problem for the Church that we must address if we are to build healthy, leader-producing cultures.

When we look to the Scripture, it won't take long to see that the people of God are a people who believe that God has revealed Himself to mankind and that mankind has the capacity to understand God's revelation. These simple truths are central to a church's understanding about reality and truth. The saints of God have an epistemology that relies on divine revelation. God reveals what can be known as true.

It is belief and trust in the person and work of Christ on the believer's behalf that makes one a Christian. Christians hold and trust these truths because their assumption is that God reveals truth and this revelation is found within Scripture.[4] It's circular logic to be sure, but such is the nature of the assumption! The Church is not judging whether the Scripture is truth, but is rather judging the truth of everything else on the basis of Scripture's truth. The people of God's Church must bleed this conviction if we are ever to produce leaders according to God's design. Without a people deeply rooted in trusting in God's revelation, there is no authority in God's Word. Without God's Word as our authority, there is no mission or mandate for the Church at all.

The insidious alternative to this conviction appeals to our human egos. It is rare to find people in American society today who do not embrace the thinking of mankind's capacity to discover truth through reason, the senses, or other natural abilities. But God's people must hold to the doctrine of revelation, or else the authority of our claims is rendered powerless.

Money, marriage, sexuality, pluralism, and so many other issues are at the forefront of the cultural conversation. How can our church prevail against the headwinds of contemporary attacks on the biblical worldview? Only a conviction that God's Word is true can keep the Church moving forward according to God's design.

If the loudest voices in the world say the Church is losing ground, falling apart, or stuck in the past, who can say any different? The Word of God says different. God's Word is, for the Church, the only definitive voice concerning His world. The Church of God will continue to be faithful to her mission to multiply disciples and leaders as long as she trusts in God's Word. The local church cannot see the making of disciples and the developing of leaders merely as a good suggestion or a clever strategy. If God's Word tells us to relentlessly develop leaders, do we trust His Word?

Ministry Urgency (time and space): Who in the world would think our beliefs on the nature of time and space would make any difference in whether a church will develop leaders? Churches make decisions about what to prioritize, how fast to move, how much money to save, and many more critical decisions as a result of their beliefs about time and space. Urgency for leadership development is built on three convictions concerning time and space: *the shortness of this life, the length of the next life,* and *the view of physical space.* Without these beliefs, urgency will be nothing more than momentary rallies to activity, and risk will be labeled as foolishness over time. To be a church culture that commits itself to the task of developing leaders, a sense of urgency must permeate the air and an appetite for wise risk must be viewed as a signpost of faith.

So what does the Bible teach us about *the shortness of this life?* The Bible's perspective is that the span of mortal human life is very, very brief—like "smoke that appears for a little while, then vanishes" (James 4:14). The Bible teaches humans have a fragile and short life on this earth, which stands in stark contrast to the eternality of God.[5] When we consider this mortal life compared to eternity, we find our lives but a solitary mark on a time line that stretches past galaxies a billion light-years away. The brevity of this life brings a sense of speed to the lives of the people of God in the local church. David expressed this perspective:

> "LORD, reveal to me the end of my life
> and the number of my days.
> Let me know how short-lived I am.
> You, indeed, have made my days short in length,
> and my life span as nothing in Your sight.
> Yes, every mortal man is only a vapor."
> (Ps. 39:4–5)

While our lives are short here, we must recognize that *the length of the next life* is everlasting. As John Newton wrote in his song "Amazing Grace": "When we've been there ten thousand years, bright shining as the sun. We've no less days to sing God's praise, than when we've first begun."[6] In this sense, the Christian paradigm of time is split. For the Church of God, it is critical to recognize time as quite brief in this life and incomprehensibly long in the next.

Every organizational culture has a perspective on distances and spaces, both actual and relative.[7] Churches are no different. A church's view of *physical space* impacts their leadership development culture. Much can be learned about church culture from the physical worship space, but the broader question concerns the local church's view concerning the "sacredness" of space in general. A church, for example, who only views the "church sanctuary" as sacred will be much more likely to fixate leadership development on leading in that environment.

At the advent of the first Christian church, believers are seen not confining their worship to the temple in Jerusalem. Their view of the sacredness of space was broader than the temple.

> Every day they devoted themselves to meeting together in the temple complex, and broke bread from house to house. They ate their food with a joyful and humble attitude, praising God and having favor with all the people. And every day the Lord added to them those who were being saved. (Acts 2:46–47)

The temple was not rejected, but neither did it serve as a constraint. The believers, recently indwelt by the Spirit of God, gained an expanded view of worship with regard to space. Worship and Kingdom activity was happening in every location the believers went! As one New Testament scholar comments, "Jesus champions neither Jerusalem nor Gerizim, 'for the hour is coming'—the eschatological hour, initiating the new age of the Kingdom of

God—when worship of the Father will be tied to no place."[8] Jesus reoriented the Church's perspective on space when He reversed the picture of the Kingdom from moving toward Jerusalem to moving out from Jerusalem to every people, tongue, and nation.[9]

For the community of faith, we must long to see the worship of God expanding out from our churches. As people indwelled by the Spirit of God, the gospel of Jesus is no longer just a "come and see" faith, but now, also, a "go and tell" faith. Who will fill the space between our local churches and the lost and dying world? The leaders we develop must!

When our churches begin to see the opportunity for ministry as truly bound only by our willingness to walk in obedience, and not bound by space, the scope of ministry changes dramatically. In light of God's revelation that His Kingdom will spread outward, our churches must look to ever-expanding horizons. The radius of ministry for the local church is only bound by the faithfulness of each of our members to go out into the world.

We can talk ourselves blue in the face about evangelism and mission, but if our churches don't fundamentally believe that God's work happens wherever God's Spirit is present, then our ministry will always come short of leader multiplication. Our passion to send leaders out is inextricably linked to the belief that God's power goes with them. If churches really believe that the people of God are empowered not only when they meet but also when they live scattered, then a conviction for developing leaders infects the culture of the church.

When the people of a congregation zealously hold convictions about time and space, the church will begin to change (and change fast)! There is a powerful grace that comes with the belief that this mortal life is terrifyingly brief and the life after death is gloriously infinite. This profound conviction moves the church to become a people of radical action, urgency, unction, and even risk.

When church leaders see their lives as undeniably fleeting, it ignites an urgency to make more leaders for God rather than to make more platforms for themselves. The *risk of not making leaders* is significantly more foolish than the risk implicit in making leaders.

Desperate and Dignified (nature of humanity): Developing leaders is incredibly hard and often quite expensive. If we don't see what God sees in mankind, we will never pay the price to unlock their true gospel-potential. However, if we don't see the sin in mankind, we will at best give them greater skills to do greater evil. For a church to have a culture of leadership development, the church must see mankind rightly.

From Genesis to Revelation, the Bible reveals that humanity has a unique place in all of creation. No other creation, according to Scripture, is declared to be "made in the image of God" and according to His "likeness of God." Man is to be more than another created thing; he is the masterpiece of all things created, he is designed to lead in creation. In the beginning, God made mankind "in a state of relative perfection, a state of righteousness and holiness."[10]

Still, between the dignity of the garden and the glory that is to come, mankind does not now seem like royal sons and daughters representing our good High King. For the introspective, it all just seems wrong. Mankind seems to be capable of so much nobility, but constantly fails to reach it. Books, songs, and movies search for answers about the nature of mankind. People inside and outside the faith wrestle with the tension we feel. Is man inherently good or evil? Can a man truly be well-intentioned? Are humans definitively corruptible? The tragic reality known to God's people holds this tension until the return of Jesus.

From the moment the Enemy tempted mankind away from obedience and trust in the Creator, mankind fell short of the glory of God and lost "something that belonged to the very nature of man in its ideal state."[11] Since that horrible day, all the descendants of Adam have carried that loss of humanity, the loss of holiness, and the loss of righteousness before their God. Every man and woman since was born and exists in a state of rebellion and depravity.[12] New Testament scholar Douglas Moo expounds on this, saying, "For the problem with people is not just that they commit sins; their problem is that they are enslaved to sin. What is needed, therefore, is a new power to break in and set people free from sin—a power found in, and only in, the gospel of Jesus Christ."[13]

People are horribly desperate. We, too, are desperate. There is no power in mortal man apart from the gracious work of God through Jesus Christ. We cover this foundational belief, this linchpin of Christian culture, because evidence shows that most churches don't buy it. Based on recent research conducted by LifeWay Research, 71 percent of Americans believe they must contribute to their own salvation.[14] We know, as William Temple aptly put, "The only thing we contribute to our salvation is the sin that makes it necessary," but the vast majority of Americans actually believe there is something they can do to save themselves. People don't believe or understand we are desperately hopeless and sinful, in need of a gracious and forgiving Savior.

If our churches are going to architect healthy and sound foundations, we cannot take any beliefs for granted. Powerlessness in a church and her leaders is a symptom of the disease of unbelief in the gospel. We are not good, we are tragically flawed—but gloriously loved, justified, and empowered by God in Christ. If our church culture seems to lack power, it is far more likely a theological issue than a strategic one. If we are to make powerful leaders in the Church, we will need to repent of leadership gimmicks and help our emerging leaders embrace the gospel.

The gospel, then, is good news for the desperate and powerless. Though the stain of sin remains for all humanity, the beauty of the gospel is that the redemption secured by Jesus offers sinful man not only forgiveness but also restoration of His image and likeness in a fuller sense.[15] This ongoing work of the Spirit in sanctification is His will to renew redeemed man "in knowledge according to the image of your Creator" (Col. 3:10). The truth of the Scripture is that mankind was made in dignity and is being restored to dignity in Jesus Christ. As men and women are restored to the image of Christ, they are connected to the power of Christ to rightly steward the leadership entrusted to them.

It may seem counterintuitive, but a basic understanding of the desperate state of fallen humanity is essential for creating a culture of leadership development. All around us, we see society attempting to highlight the best in mankind by making much of human capacity. From Oprah to The Home Depot ("you can do it, we can help"), society's message is that mankind can find greatness by looking inside themselves.

This kind of thinking has even invaded the Church. Leaders within Christian circles can be found encouraging people to believe in themselves and to hone their willpower to claim what they desire out of life (with God's blessing of course). In some ways, the Christian leaders parroting this nonsense likely do it because they want to see power unleashed through their people. No doubt humanity is capable of being used for miraculous things, but the way to access this power is a mysterious paradox. The gospel tells us that through realizing our desperate need for God, repenting of our independence and willfulness, we can witness and enjoy the majestic power of God rather than the futile power of self.

Making leaders in the local church must be an activity of training leaders to be humbly dependent, not willfully independent. Powerful leaders can be produced in a church that unabashedly embraces the powerlessness of independent man.

Still, even in light of our depravity, since all humans are made in the image of God and likeness of God, we must ascribe dignity to all men and women. This is key for developing leaders. In the

Kingdom of God there is no elite class or higher caste. Every human is capable of the highest nobility and the most profound power in Christ Jesus. Therefore, the local church develops leaders with an eye on everyone. In this sense, we can never predict through genetics or family origin who will be called to lead in God's Kingdom. For all born again in Christ have the birthright necessary to lead the Kingdom. Sadly, so often this belief is unrecognizable in the local church. Leadership teams are filled with those of great pedigree and education. A local church must not look at people through the same lens as the world.

Because sanctification is a lifelong process, churches must take the long view of potential leaders. As a church incurs the risk, and often the cost of failure, for developing leaders, a conviction concerning the power and promise of sanctification must become a hallmark of Christian development. Potential leaders in the local church may have been redeemed, but they are still undergoing renewal in this life. As Paul found out after a knock-down-drag-out with Barnabas about the usefulness of John Mark, sanctification is slow, but it is powerful.[16] As a local church hopes to build a culture of leadership development, it will be forced to extend its development horizon and expand its faith in God's power to renew.

The Household of God

For any organizational culture there is a set of beliefs that tells members who they are, how members ought to interact, and who is a part of the group. The local church is not different in that regard. Building on assumptions about the realities of creation, the local church must share a set of convictions about cooperation within the body. The results in church culture that embraces the beauty of belonging to God's household will be expressed in *oneness, ownership,* and *accountability.*

Oneness. If a church is to build a culture that develops leaders, she must have clarity around her sense of self. The most impressive organizations in the world at developing leaders develop them out of a deep sense of belonging to something greater than themselves. Whether it is the armed forces or prestigious universities, a strong sense of belonging with connection to a storied heritage is essential for the development of future leaders. Humans, especially leaders, are drawn to glory. We crave belonging to something with gravity. This instinct, we think, is a remnant of our design. So, to pursue a strong culture, capable of producing leaders, we want future leaders to feel the weight of being one with the household of God.

The believer in Christ is now adopted into the family of God as a son or daughter. This is no illustration, but is reality:

> All those who are led by God's Spirit are God's sons. For you did not receive a spirit of slavery to fall back into fear, but you received the Spirit of adoption, by whom we cry out, "Abba, Father!" (Rom. 8:14–15)

This passage not only reveals the intimacy of belonging to God's household, but also reminds us that God's people are legal members in the family of God and, therefore, coheirs with Christ.[17] This reality entitles all sons and daughters to all the duties, rights, and privileges associated with being a child in God's Kingdom.[18] This truth should never cease to stun us. The local church that develops leaders does so as a father or mother would invest in a child. We are not producing minions, or even legions of soldiers for the Kingdom of God. We are training family.

So what is the family business?

Well, it's ruling. God has designed mankind to lead, which He is now doing through His Son as the Head of the Church. If you belong to a local church then you are in the family business. Our business is to be ambassadors of our Father's Kingdom. An ambassador is a citizen of one country representing that country in a foreign land, and Scripture is clear about this identity for those who are in Christ. The local church is made up of believers who, by extension of their oneness with Christ, work together as ambassadors for Christ. Every believer in the local church ought to feel the weight of belonging to a unified family serving as ambassadors. There are no believers in our churches who are not, by identity, engaged in the work of God's new glorious Kingdom. Advancing the rule and reign of God is not just something some believers *do*; rather it is a part of the *identity* of what it means to be His. A church culture aiming to build leaders must have a unity around its most fundamental identity. The local church is to make leaders, as a family, to be ambassadors (2 Cor. 5:17–20).

In every church culture there are a number of shared metaphors that build the basis for cooperation among members in God's household. Metaphors, in fact, are one of the most powerful tools in forming cultures. Sometimes metaphors are created by individual local churches to help solidify the church in special ways. Other metaphors ought to be shared across all local churches because they are the very words of Scripture. One such metaphor found in Scripture is the Church as the "body of Christ" (1 Cor. 12:12). This metaphor demonstrates that there is a profound unity in the local church coupled with a distinct diversity. Gordon Fee captures this unity and diversity well:

> The body is one, yet the body has many members. In saying that it is one, his concern is for its essential unity. But that does not mean uniformity. That was the Corinthian error, to think that uniformity was a value, or that it represented true spirituality. Paul's concern is for their unity; but there is no such thing as true unity without diversity.[19]

The metaphor of the body also leads the believer to understand that this unity in Christ and with each other is unbreakable.[20] No matter how critical any part is in the body, no part can survive without the others. The metaphor of the body informs the church of the need for each part to cooperate to maintain the health and growth of the body.[21] The body only functions properly when each part bears its proper role, which is a gift for the good of the whole body (Eph. 4:11–13).

To help bind a church in "oneness," church leaders are wise to employ the use of shared words and concepts. An investigation into the most important words and concepts of the local church will reveal much about its identity. For developing leaders, if the most important words don't point to equipping and developing saints for ministry, no amount of structure or programming will overcome it. As with any culture, the unity of the movement is partially preserved and propagated by shared vocabulary and sets of ideas. For many cultures, it is difficult for the leaders to get traction with new ideas because they lack clarity in language. Leader-developing culture can be destroyed or undermined by confusion among members concerning important words and concepts. We rarely think about things like this, but we cannot have a cohesive, reproducing culture if we don't have shared language. Words and concepts such as "Scripture/Bible," "Salvation/Saved," "Mission," "Gospel," "Church," "Great Commission," and "Great Commandment" can mean a variety of things to different people. For us to have any success in developing future leaders, it is critical that we are speaking the same language with the same definitions underneath the common language. Common language, with common understanding, is essential for oneness. Oneness is essential for a culture developing leaders.

If this oneness can be fostered and expressed, the local church can be one of the most fertile places for developing the future leaders of the church and society. The sense of identity and belonging are not just attractive benefits for developing leaders in a church, they are powerful in making them into the leaders they will become. While the Scripture needs no validation regarding the reality of oneness in the Church, significant research in the field of leadership development reinforces the claim that this sense of belonging and group identity are crucial to the task of leadership formation.[22]

There is a power for developing leaders that comes with believing that we belong to one another. Can you imagine if someone were to develop you as if you were "one" with him or her? The mystery of our union with Christ is that we now belong to Christ and to one another. Like no organization in the world, a church's care for emerging leaders is founded on a relationship of sacrifice and love.

Ownership. We cannot build strong cultures if we don't know who is in and who is out. The primary language used by the New Testament in reference to members of the Church is "in Christ." Scripture is remarkably clear that those truly "in Christ" have the indwelling presence of the Spirit of God. A covenantal relationship is formed through the new birth; Jesus is bound to His Church, and church members are bound to one another.[23] This binding covenant between the members of a local church propels them to consider the community over self. This dedication and loyalty in the body of Christ creates the environment for spending oneself in an effort to bless future generations with new and capable leadership. Without the fundamental belief that we ought to sacrifice ourselves for others, leadership development is reduced to a common pyramid scheme rather than holy multiplication. We can't expect to bear the fruit of godly new leaders if our local church is not faithful to operate properly as God's household.

Throughout the New Testament, the local church is told to act and believe in a number of ways toward one another. The command to "love one another" appears eight times in the New Testament alone and is reiterated using different language. In the midst of a long list of prescriptive interactions among believers, Paul writes to the Colossians, "Above all, put on love—the perfect bond of unity"

(Col. 3:14). He is not saying that love is to be put on instead of all the other ways to interact properly with the people of God, but rather that love ought to be pursued as an ultimate expression of all those things. The assertion that "God is love" does not mean that love is merely one of His attributes or actions, but that all He does is loving.[24] If all of God's activity is love, and the household of God is to be a reflection of His divine image and activity, then so also must all of our activity be characterized by love. It is this conviction in the local church that sets her apart from all others in the capacity to produce leaders.

We love God, so we love His Church. We love His Church, so we want to provide her with the best leadership possible. We love emerging leaders because they are part of ourselves, and our Lord, through union with Christ. This chain of love creates the most powerful platform for leadership development in our societies.

A belief in membership is woefully incomplete without a strong belief in the priesthood of all believers. Every person who belongs to Him is a priest (1 Pet. 2:9), with access to God and responsibility to minister with His authority.[25] Through the work of Christ, every member of the local church is included in the ministry of God.[26] With every act done in the name of Jesus and by the power of the Spirit, the delegated authority of God is exercised over creation. Thus, the ministry of the saints is the power of God undoing the effects of sin in the world.[27] Therefore, as the local church mobilizes the membership to utilize their power in Jesus, every member is an agent of the Kingdom. Without an abiding conviction in members as powerful agents of the Kingdom, leadership development will only be a task in delegation rather than empowerment.

As the local church embraces a biblical view of church membership, a powerful expression in the church is unlocked: ownership. People treat rental cars much differently than cars they own, and people treat a church they "just rent" much differently than one where they "own the mission." Pastors and church leaders aim for "buy-in" and "involvement," but what they really long for is own-ership. When we turn the pages of Scripture, we are forced to deal with a God who demands utter and absolute commitment to His ways and His cause. We are desperate for this radical ownership to be the mark of our local churches. As our church members embrace the beauty of mutual oneness and ownership in the local body, they move from "renting" or "borrowing" the mission they hear the preachers preaching and internalize the mission as their own.

When ownership of God's vision and God's mission is the water our members swim in, there will be a great swell of emerging leaders desperate to be equipped for the task. Without ownership, our leadership development will be subjected to the futility of beg-ging people to "step up" and minimizing the expectations to make sure it "isn't asking too much of people." Could you imagine the Army worrying itself on the battlefield about telling soldiers the importance of the mission? Could you imagine how development would be effected if the Army worried its training efforts were "asking too much"? Ownership in the local church is the permis-sion the body gives developers to push them to be the best leaders they can be in Christ.

Accountability. In every culture and every group, people have perspective about how leadership works, how power is distributed, how decisions are made, and how new rules are created. In devel-oping new leaders it is crucial to have a significant consistency and clarity about authority and accountability. The two primary principles that capture the biblical perspective on authority in the local church are the lordship of Jesus and the understanding of "undershepherds."

The understanding of authority in the local church must be rooted in the lordship of Jesus. The Church is fundamentally a theocracy, ruled and led by Jesus Christ Himself. Christ is on the throne over all mankind, particularly over His Church.[28] Thus all power, in all creation and in the Church, is under the active authority of Jesus. Norman Geisler expounds on the extent of Jesus' authority:

> Christ is not only the invisible Head of the invisible universal church (see Eph. 1:22–23), He is also the invisible Head of the visible local church(es). This is made clear in Revelation, where He stands in their midst as Lord over them.[29]

Those of us who live in America are not naturally inclined to monarchy. We attempt to democratize every institution to which we belong. However, if the local church is going to produce biblical leaders, they must first be submitted followers of King Jesus. The local church is the most profound expression on this earth of a submitted creation to the Sovereign King of the universe. We will only produce tyrants and charlatans (albeit clothed sometimes like clergy) if our churches are not grounded in the lordship of Jesus over all things.

A church's belief about the authority of "undershepherds" also shapes the culture. The term itself captures the subordinated and delegated nature of the authority of those God entrusts to lead the church. Undershepherd is most appropriately applied to those called "elder" or "pastor." Speaking to elders, the apostle Peter says:

> Therefore, as a fellow elder and witness to the sufferings of the Messiah and also a participant in the glory about to be revealed, I exhort the elders among you: Shepherd God's flock among you, not overseeing out of compulsion but freely, according to God's will; not for the money but eagerly; not lording it over those entrusted to you, but being examples to the flock. And when the chief Shepherd appears, you will receive the unfading crown of glory. (1 Pet. 5:1–4)

Peter's words capture the basic nature of the authority given to the undershepherds of God. The elder, nor anyone speaking for Christ, has any authority apart from leadership that advances the will of God, which is clearly and authoritatively recorded in the Scriptures. Therefore, the authority of the elder is confined by and inseparable from the authority of the revealed words of God in the Bible.[30] Accordingly, the members of the local church honor the leadership of their undershepherds as an expression of their trust in the Word of God. Jonathan Leeman says, "Christians don't join churches; they submit to them."[31] The submission to this leadership looks more like submission within a family than anything else. But, as a family, a church thrives when love is accomplished through truth, accountability, discipline, care, and protection.

The undershepherd is chiefly a steward. The Church belongs to One, and none of us are Him. Scripture is clear that elders should constantly bear in mind that "the flock does not belong to them and that they are therefore undershepherds entrusted with another's possessions."[32] The flock entrusted to the elders is now, and forever will be, the flock of God. This not only applies to leaders in the Church, but also to those who would lead any people, as all people belong to God.

In the local church, leaders are not leading "their people," they are leading "God's people." This understanding creates accountability between the local church leaders and God Himself. We lead God's people how He wants them led. If God wants His people trained and equipped to lead according to His design, then the Church is beholden to obey.

The Mission of God

Just as every organization and church has a foundational set of beliefs about how the members ought to interact with each other, so also they have beliefs about how to interact with those outside themselves. A local church needs to have a shared understanding as to why the local church exists and what she is called to do. Church after church sits idle and aging because the mission of God is not front and center. However, if we are to build leaders according to God's design, we must bring acute clarity to our convictions. A necessary theological conviction for the leader-developing church is a people deeply *devoted to the glory of God and dedicated to multiplication.*

Devoted to the glory of God. A local church culture is shaped significantly by assumptions about its purpose. If we miss on the purpose of God's people, we will miss entirely. Beginning with Genesis, God's design for creation is to share in and manifest His glory, for He made humanity in His image and His likeness to be the crowning jewel of His creation. The local church, made up of redeemed mankind, headed by Christ, united by the indwelling of the Spirit of Christ, now has the purpose of inaugurating the restoring of God's matchless glory throughout all creation. If a church is to become all that she was made to be, she must hold in highest regard her calling to do all for the glory of God.

There are many ways a church culture can truly and rightly bring glory to God. The faith of the saints under pressure, suffering, and persecution brings attention to the worth and value of King Jesus. Our perseverance on this long road to glory honors Him. Our joyful obedience to Him magnifies His worth to a watching world. All of these things and more make God's Church a glory-reflecting community that honors the Eternal God.

A firm conviction that the Church exists to bring God glory makes a local church immensely powerful for developing new leaders. The glory-hogging of leaders deeply hampers leadership development. Leaders filled with pride fail to develop others as they fear others surpassing them, others receiving credit, or others "stealing the spotlight." The glory of God slays the glory of man. A church obsessed with the glory of God continually defeats the Enemy that threatens to stall the maturation of new leaders. As the local church embraces the glory of God, new leaders can rise up, new leaders can pass their mentors, and old leaders can step aside in dignity and delight. What a wonderful reality. Our dedication to the glory of God and self-forgetfulness brings our churches into a deep, powerful devotion. This kind of devotion can help us remain dedicated to developing new leaders even if it means loss of power or glory for self. There is nothing so liberating, so freeing, as replacing your own leadership as an act of worship to God.

Dedicated to multiplication. In these last days, God has determined to use His Church as His primary agent in ushering in His Kingdom. This reality is made clear to God's people throughout Scripture, but pointedly in the Great Commission.[33] Jesus makes His mandate clear; we are to advance His Kingdom by making disciples. That's it—we want to make much of Jesus through advancing His reign by declaring and demonstrating the gospel and instructing others to join us.

The mission of the local church is not up for debate. The mission of the Church is the mission of the One who is the Head of the Church. Namely, His particular mission is "to seek and to save the lost" (Luke 19:10). A church joins in that mission or she is no body of Christ.

How will the local church know when it has accomplished or is succeeding in its mission? This question must be answered by all organizations, and the local church is no exception. Strong cultures have clarity when it comes to mission. Unity falls apart and mission falters when there is no clarity on success. This has been particularly true in American churches. The American local church regularly communicates particular measurements, such as budgets and buildings, that frame the perspective of new members concerning the mission. Christ, however, has clearly identified for the Church the end of the mission, the point of the mission, and the accomplishment of the mission:

> "This good news of the kingdom will be proclaimed in all the world as a testimony to all nations. And then the end will come." (Matt. 24:14)

Do we believe that budgets and Sunday attendance is enough to measure progress in the mission of reaching all nations? We will (at best) get only what we aim for. If our local churches are ever to become the epicenter of leadership development, then they must fully embrace the mission and its massive scope. For the local church to fully accept responsibility for the mission of God to be completed, developing leaders will be a necessary ambition. For most churches, the problem of mission is not they have aimed too big, but that they have aimed way too small.

Churches must measure leadership reproduction because if leaders are not being made, the church has been unfaithful. As the local church embraces the mission of making disciples, she will be unlocked for her fullest potential in multiplication. The local church must see leadership development as an expression of obedience to the Great Commission. Leaders cannot simply make more followers of Christ; they must be intent on replacing themselves as leaders. The multiplication of disciples and churches is significantly tied to the multiplication of leaders. If a local church embraces the mission to make disciples of all nations, then there is no other palatable strategy but to make more leaders to press the mission forward.

Convictions and Culture

If churches are to build a healthy culture for developing leaders, they cannot simply correct behavior and change programs. Behavior is an expression of the church's underlying beliefs, so addressing behavior alone will prove insufficient. Neither can a church simply reorganize their way to a healthy culture. We must cultivate the theological assumptions beneath the surface. The task of culture cultivation must be taken seriously. We cannot expect a harvest if we are planting seeds in barren soil.

If a church's convictions are consistent with Scripture, the church will see the fruit revealed in Scripture. If a church's convictions are inconsistent with a biblical worldview, she will continue to struggle. In order to develop a strong leadership culture, a church must follow the design of Scripture. Just as God has designed mankind to lead, He has designed His Church to equip His people to lead.

We praise God for the work He is doing through churches that measure more than finances and attendance. For The Summit Church, the theologically cultivated culture has produced leaders well beyond the church. In the last thirteen years the church has launched 9 campuses, planted 93 churches, sent 333 long-term missionaries, and continually trains hundreds of marketplace leaders. We rejoice that churches are not merely *dismissing* their members at the conclusion of their worship gatherings, but instead they are constantly reminding God's people that they are *sent*.

Theology and church culture are more interwoven than most leaders have assumed. What a church really believes, not just what they say they believe, impacts how leaders are developed.

Since culture is so important, can a culture be changed? Turn the page. . . .

CHAPTER
SIX

Transforming Culture

It is easier to kill an organization than it is to change it.
—Tom Peters

Every gathering of people, every organization has a culture. Though a local church is much more than *just* an organization, every church has a culture. Some church cultures are healthy and some are unhealthy, but every church has a culture. Healthy church cultures are conducive for leadership development. They don't merely say they value leadership development; they actually believe the Church is responsible to develop and deploy leaders, and they align their actions to this deeply held conviction.

Culture ultimately begins with the actual beliefs and values that undergird all the actions and behavior. A church's capacity for developing leaders relies on the collective worldview of the church and whether it is compatible with the ambition. A church's culture has the power to significantly impede or empower its effectiveness in the Great Commission and the call to multiplication. Leaders create culture and culture shapes leaders and churches, even without recognizing it. Ministry leaders must understand the transformative power of culture if they want to have mature communities of faith.[1]

Organizational culture, and more pertinently church culture, is intensely potent. Church culture is a powerful force in the hands of those who shape a local church according to God's design. If you are reading this book in any type of building, rebar is likely holding the building up and connecting the structure together. Glance up from the book and look for the rebar (short for reinforcing bar). You can't see it, but it is impacting everything you see. You often can't see culture, not in the same way you can see the doctrinal statement (the expressed convictions) or the leadership pipeline (the expressed constructs), but it holds everything in place. For better or worse, culture impacts your church more than you often realize.

Building on the expert work of Edgar Schein, church culture can be seen in three layers, each layer building and depending on the layer below it.[2] These layers move from actual beliefs to articulated beliefs, to the expression of those beliefs (called artifacts). All three layers make up the culture in a church.

LAYERS OF
CHURCH CULTURE

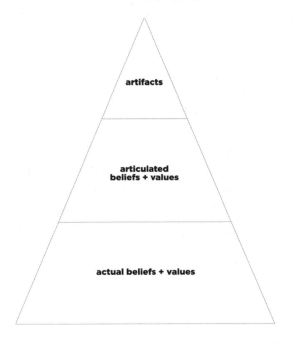

artifacts

articulated
beliefs + values

actual beliefs + values

Actual beliefs are what the group collectively believes, not merely *says* they believe. In his acclaimed work *Built to Last*, Jim Collins describes the culture of "visionary companies." Two of the four traits he observed in the culture of great companies are related to their actual beliefs. A strong culture has, according to Collins, a fervently held ideology and indoctrination of that ideology.[3] Surely a company should not have a more fervently held ideology than a local body of believers. Surely a company should not be more passionate about indoctrination than a local church.

While not everything that is articulated is really believed, what is really believed is always *articulated*. If something is really valued, it is declared. Language and words help create the culture one lives in. When the Babylonians, for example, took Daniel and his contemporaries into captivity, they schooled the people of God in their language and literature (Dan. 1:4). The Babylonian leaders knew the power of words, both spoken and read, in attempting to form culture. The articulated beliefs and even *how* they are articulated help form the culture. How a church speaks of those outside the church, of the Scripture, and of the mission influences the culture greatly.

The *artifacts* of church culture are the visible, tangible expressions of a church's actual and articulated beliefs. Artifacts include common behaviors, informal rules for interaction, and other customs. Artifacts also include the formal behavioral management systems like policies, organizational structures, meeting formats, and required procedures. Church cultures even express their beliefs through artifacts that are nonhuman. Our buildings, technology, art, music, and other resources and tools constitute expression of our culture. Our programs and church calendars are expressions of who we are and are embedded in our cultures. Artifacts reveal a church's worldview and simultaneously shape the church to continue believing it.

The artifacts are often what people latch on to most in a church, though they are expressions of so much beneath the surface. Imagine growing up in a healthy church. The church is generous, kind, nurturing, full of truth, and loving. You grow up loving your church. This church happens to have some programs that have deeply impacted you. Maybe it was a children's program or a great worship ministry. In your mind, even without realizing it, your affinity for belief of the church is connected to the visible expressions of the church. Now, years long past that first church experience, artifacts that seem nearest to those original expressions will just feel right. Because of this, people are often really attached to the artifacts. While changing actual beliefs is the most difficult task, changing artifacts often creates the most pain.

In order to understand culture, it is critical to recognize the differences in the layers. It is faster to correct unwanted behaviors or artifacts in a culture, but only addressing behavior is insufficient. Unless all the layers of culture are addressed, other deviant behaviors will pop up in the place of recently addressed ones.

This game of behavioral whack-a-mole becomes an endless cycle of battling unnamed enemies underneath the surface. The unwanted behaviors are symptoms; an unhealthy culture is the sickness. Wherever we find stubborn sticking points in a church culture, there is always inconsistency between the actual beliefs and values and the stated ones. If there are deeply held assumptions and beliefs within the culture that are incompatible with the desired future that leaders are leading toward, then the beliefs beneath the surface must be addressed.

If our churches are going to have strong cultures, there must be actual beliefs driven deeply into the church that are articulated and then expressed in artifacts. There will be harmony and congruence between all three layers of culture. The church won't settle for mere alignment between the *articulated* values and the *artifacts*. The leaders will push for the *actual* beliefs to be deeply rooted in the church. The true beliefs and assumptions of a church culture are not only written on signs, posters, and e-mail footers. The truly embraced convictions of a local church are written in the lives of believers as they interact with one another and the world.

Church leaders often mistakenly think of church culture as primarily a combination between *articulated beliefs* and the *expressions of those beliefs*. By doing so, leaders fail to look deeper to the first layer of culture. They fail to grasp the *actual beliefs* and *actual shared values* beneath the surface. Too many church leaders are betting the farm that church culture is a simple matter of "what we say" plus "what we do." The strategy for changing culture, if this was the case, is then quite simple: If we don't like what people are doing, then we simply need to say something different. This tragic error assigns organizational culture (and changing it) to the power of positive thinking and some form of "name it and claim it" theology. For the observant, there is likely a nagging suspicion that church culture, and the way to change, is something more. Culture is much more than what we say and do. Culture is formed by what we truly believe and value over a sustained period of time. If the stated beliefs of a church are at odds with the actual beliefs, the actual beliefs win. The actual yet unstated beliefs speak louder than the stated ones, if the two are at odds. Some examples may be helpful.

If the stated doctrine of the church is that all believers are priests and ministers because our great High Priest has made us priests through His death, yet the culture of the church values only "professional ministers"—the culture will trump the doctrinal confession. A pastor preaching Ephesians 4:11–12 one time will not automatically remove the unrealistic and unbiblical expectation that the pastor is the one who *does* the ministry.

If a stated belief of the church is that no one has anything to offer to stand holy before God, yet the actual beliefs are that we somehow contribute to our standing with God by our religious goodness, the culture will be one that does not allow for openness and confession. And someone who admits a struggle will be unlikely to experience mercy expressed from another. A graceless culture overpowers a grace-filled confessional statement.

If the stated doctrine of the church is that we are to live as missionaries because Jesus stepped into our culture to rescue us, but the culture of the church focuses almost exclusively on what programs and events the church offers, the culture will attempt to squelch and suffocate desires to serve the surrounding community.

Time and time again a little digging reveals that the outcomes of the local church contradict the ambitious vision statements. Why is this so? Why don't our campaigns, rebranding efforts, and endless streams of mission statements change our future?

These undesirable outcomes and behaviors exist because there is a mission-killing divergence between *what we say our church believes* and what our *church actually believes.* When the theological statements and catchy slogans don't match the theological convictions actually held by the people of the local church, the God-honoring hopes of that church will never become a reality. It is for this reason that many churches who want to engage in leadership development can't seem to get the church to fall in line. The strategy of "program cut-and-paste" will not serve our local churches in creating the actual change needed. All three layers of culture must be continually considered. In order to become churches that embrace the call to produce leaders, we have to take a hard and thoughtful look at our church culture.

Diagnosing Actual Beliefs

Managing church culture is ultimately a pastoral function. This is not a tool for pragmatists or a skill set borrowed from business. Engaging in the fight for healthy church culture is fighting for faith for God's people. Serving to cultivate healthy church culture in a local church is the regular work of uncovering disbelief or wrong belief among God's people and working to commend true faith to God's people. Church disbelief must be transformed.

Is there such a thing as organizational or church disbelief? Can a whole group disbelieve? Yes! In the same way that some societies are riddled by disbelief in the gospel because of an intertwining of some false religion and the worldview of a people group, so also churches can have systemic false beliefs. In modern-day Turkey, for example, many converts to Christ will remark on the difficulty of believing the gospel as a Turk, largely because of the false belief that to be a Turk is to be a Muslim. For Turks, being a follower of Christ is inconsistent with the worldview of being a Turk. There are whole societies in the world, including churches, that have distinct errors in their thinking that are held by a majority of the people.

The leaders of God's Church must approach church culture as a doctor caring for the patient but wanting to remove the sickness from the body. God's leaders must diagnose the widespread errors in belief that are harming the body from inside our church cultures. It is these widespread errors in worldview that often account for unhealthy culture in the local church. Leading culture in the local church is leading a whole church to purity in doctrine and in deed.

For a leader to diagnose a church for a culture compatible for developing leaders requires a good bit of courage and even more humility. The leadership task of discovering problems rather than ignoring them is not necessarily a well-worn path in the world of Christian leadership. We struggle to admit something is off or wrong in our cultures. For many, "ministry success" is the only acceptable narrative, and the demand for it has been fertile soil for hubris that has plagued leaders longing for or envious of ministry celebrity status. But if we are to be churches that train the very best leaders, we must put our egos to death. For the leader who longs for the church to repent, change often begins with *the leader's* repentance.

While we are wasting our time if we only address behavior while ignoring the wrong convictions, to discover what a culture fundamentally believes, a leader must work backward from the behaviors. While it is foolish and futile to attempt to change culture by only addressing behavior, one can learn the culture by watching the collective behavior of the church, by observing what is applauded and what is seen as normal. By observing the aggregate behaviors of the people, one can get a good sense of what the church really believes.

We offer the following framework to help church leaders assess if the culture actually believes in and values leadership development. While this list of attributes does not cover everything that can or should be present in a church culture, we believe this list includes critical cultural attributes necessary for leadership development. The framework was built from the theological beliefs outlined in the previous chapter along with potential deviant expressions that corrode a church culture. As you consider your church culture, do the attributes on the left describe the church or those on the right?

CULTURAL FOUNDATIONS:
WHAT'S AT STAKE?

ASSOCIATED CONVICTION	DESIRED EXPRESSIONS	DEVIANT EXPRESSIONS
realities of creation	trust in God's Word urgency + risk honor + humility	opinionated + subjective apathetic + low priority on training powerless, elitest, or harsh
household of God	oneness ownership accountability	loveless duty + grumbling service indifference + transactional domineering or unchallenging
mission of God	devotion multiplication	inward-focused + self-protecting manipulation + selfishness

Working backward from the behavioral analysis, it is possible to make some theological assessments for church culture. For churches that observe behaviors from the list on the right, this is a strong indication that the associated convictions are not consistently held within the body. Leaders are often surprised when these deviant behaviors manifest, especially in a church with strong, biblical doctrinal and mission statements. We, as leaders, often assume that the things we hold dear transfer by osmosis to our church members. Sadly, it just doesn't work this way. For example, many evangelical churches pride themselves on having a robust theology and conviction about the immanent return of Christ. And, if a majority of members in one of these churches was asked how they should live in light of that conviction, many would say something like, "I should live ready for His return any day." Yet the same church may demonstrate consistently a lack of urgency. How can this be? Simple. People don't always really believe what they say they believe. There is often disparity between actual beliefs and articulated ones.

These cultural inconsistencies are pervasive and no church is immune. At Austin Stone, where Kevin serves as lead pastor, there was a time at the start of the church when this truth became so clear. For years, the leadership team talked about the call of every Christian to be a part of the mission of God. Yet, when looking deeply at the church, something was not quite right. The worship services were growing, but impact in the city was not.

The team knew it needed more than just a sermon, more than just a class or a strategy. The church needed a cultural change. The Austin Stone was certain that God was calling her to be a church for the city of Austin, but teaching a list of "dos and don'ts" wasn't going to get her there.[4] The seeds for a city-loving, God-honoring church were in there, but until God altered some of the fundamental beliefs as a local church, nothing would have changed. The church needed to really believe the urgency of the mission, needed to really believe that the Lord was inviting His people to join Him on mission in all spheres of life.

Culture change is key. Without cultural change, we are hopeless to change existing results.[5] Of all changes, cultural change is the most difficult. It is essentially changing the collective DNA of an entire group of people. To understand how to change culture, it is helpful to know how change works in general.

Changing Church Culture

Change is extremely difficult. One of the most vivid and striking examples of this painful reality is the inability of heart patients to change even when confronted with grim reality. Roughly six hundred thousand people have a heart bypass each year in the United States. These patients are told they must change. They must change their eating habits, must exercise, and quit smoking and drinking. If they do not, they will die. The case for change is so compelling that they are literally told, "Change or die."[6] Yet despite the clear instructions and painful reality, 90 percent of the patients do not change. Within two years of hearing such brutal facts, they remain the same. Change is *that* challenging for people. For the vast majority of patients, death is chosen over change.

Yet leadership is often about change, about moving a group of people to a new future. Perhaps the most recognized leadership book on leading an organization to change is John Kotter's *Leading Change*. And when ministry leaders speak or write about leadership, they often look to the wisdom found in the book of Nehemiah, as it chronicles Nehemiah's leadership in rebuilding the wall around Jerusalem. Nehemiah led wide-scale change. Nehemiah never read Kotter's book, and he led well without it. The Lord well equipped Nehemiah for the task of leading God's people. But it is fascinating to see how Nehemiah's actions mirror much of what Kotter has observed in leaders who successfully lead change. With a leadership development culture in mind, here are the eight steps for leading change, according to Kotter, and how one can see them in Nehemiah's leadership.

1. Establish a sense of urgency. Leaders must create dissatisfaction with an ineffective status quo. They must help others develop a sense of angst over the brokenness around them. Nehemiah heard a negative report from Jerusalem, and it crushed him to the point of weeping, fasting, and prayer (Neh. 1:3–4). Sadly, the horrible situation in Jerusalem had become the status quo. The disgrace did not bother the people in the same way that it frustrated Nehemiah. After he arrived in Jerusalem, he walked around and observed the destruction. Before he launched the vision of rebuilding the wall, Nehemiah pointed out to the people that they were in trouble and ruins. He started with urgency, not vision. Without urgency, plans for change do not work.

If you assess your culture and find deviant behaviors that reveal some inaccurate theological beliefs, you must create urgency by pointing these out. If you assess your culture and find a lack of leadership development, a sense of urgency must be created. Leadership development is an urgent matter because the mission the Lord has given us is so great.

2. Form a guiding coalition. Effectively leading change requires a community of people, a group aligned on mission and values and committed to the future of the organization. Nehemiah enlisted the wisdom and help of others. He invited others to participate in leading the effort to rebuild the wall.

As you diagnose the culture in your church, do not lead alone. Change will not happen with one lone voice. It is foolish for leaders to attempt to lead alone, and insanity for leaders to attempt to lead change alone.

3. Develop a vision and strategy. Vision attracts people and drives action. Without owning and articulating a compelling vision for the future, leaders are not leading. The vision Nehemiah articulated to the people was simple and compelling: "Let us rebuild the wall of Jerusalem, and we will no longer be in disgrace." Nehemiah wisely rooted the action of building the wall with visionary language: "We are the people of God and should not be in disgrace."

The vision to build leaders is more challenging than building a wall, but the motivation is the same: "We are the people of God. We must spread His fame to all spheres of life and to the ends of the earth."

4. Communicate the vision. Possessing a vision for change is not sufficient; the vision must be communicated effectively. Without great communication, a vision is a mere dream. Nehemiah communicated the vision personally through behavior and to others through his words. Besides his communication, Nehemiah embodied the vision. His commitment to it was clear to all. He traveled many miles and risked much to be in Jerusalem instigating change. He continued to press on toward the completion of the vision despite ridicule (Neh. 6:3). Vision is stifled when the leader preaches something different than he lives.

If a church is going to effectively communicate the vision to develop and deploy leaders, this vision must own the leaders. It must compel you to personally pour your life into others.

5. Empower others to act. Leaders seek to empower others and deploy them for action. They seek to remove obstacles that hamper action that is in line with the vision. The rebuilding of the wall was a monumental task that took many people; therefore, it required broadening the base of those committed to the vision. Nehemiah involved many people in the project. He placed people in areas about which they were passionate. For example, several worked on the wall in front of their homes (3:23), likely most burdened for that particular area of the wall.

Ministry leaders must empower others to develop leaders. Leadership development must not be only the responsibility of the senior pastor or senior leadership team. Others must be invited to embrace the opportunity to invest their lives in creating and commissioning leaders.

6. Generate short-term wins. Change theorist William Bridges stated, "Quick successes reassure the believers, convince the doubters, and confound the critics."[7] Leaders are wise to secure early wins to leverage momentum. Nehemiah and those rebuilding the wall faced immediate and constant ridicule and opposition; therefore, it was necessary for Nehemiah to utilize short-term wins to maintain momentum. After the initial wave of criticism, Nehemiah noted that the wall was halfway complete (4:6). The reality of the progress created enough energy to overcome the onslaught of negativity.

Ministry leaders can create short-term wins by beginning with a few people, by inviting others to be developed. As leaders are discipled, people in the church will take notice. People will begin to see that the church does more than produce programs and events.

7. Consolidate improvements and produce more change. Effective change gives leaders freedom and credibility for more change. The reconstruction of the wall was one aspect of the change that Nehemiah implemented. The overriding problem was the disgrace and destruction of the people. After their return from exile, the people did not initially reinstate the worship of God and observance of the Law. Furthermore, there were numerous social injustices that were tolerated and led by the officials and nobles. The completion of the wall was, in itself, a huge short-term win. It only took fifty-two days to complete, but its impact was enormous, as surrounding nations knew it was "accomplished by our God" (6:15–16). The success of the reconstruction allowed Nehemiah to lead bolder changes under the banner of eliminating the disgrace and destruction of the people.

8. Anchor new approaches in the culture. Leaders do not create a new culture in order to make changes; instead, they make changes to create a new culture. Nehemiah inherited a culture of mediocrity, indifference, and oppression. The walls were in ruin, which made the people susceptible to attack at any time. The people were out of fellowship with God. They had lost their sense of identity as God's chosen people. Nehemiah diagnosed the culture of the people by observing their behavior. He confronted them on the incongruence between how they were living and who they said they were. "We are the people of God!" Every change led to the realization by the people that they were God's possession, that God was their protector and strength. Every aspect of the change move-ment was integrated into the unified whole of being the people of God.

As the deviant expressions of the church are diagnosed and the inaccurate actual beliefs confronted, right beliefs must be rooted in the culture. Initiating the right behaviors in a church can help change the culture, but the culture will not be crystallized unless the right behaviors are rooted in the right actual beliefs. For exam-ple, ministry leaders can initiate mission opportunities for people in the church. These right behaviors can impact the church to think externally, to love the city, to care for those outside the walls of the church. But if leaders are not simultaneously rooting the right behavior in the *why* behind the mission activity, the actual belief that the people of God are to join God on mission, then the right behaviors will be very fragile and short-lived. Don't settle for arti-fact modification; go for cultural transformation. But to get there, the right actions must be connected to the right beliefs.

Culture, in John Kotter's model, is not changed until the end of the change process. It is that challenging and that time consuming. As difficult as changing behavior is, changing church culture is even more difficult. We only need to return to Nehemiah to learn this painful reality. While he was able to lead the transforming of a wall, though he tried, he was unable to lead the transformation of the culture. A wall was constructed, but the culture was never transformed.

After the wall was rebuilt and Ezra read the Law for the first time since the captivity in Babylon, the people responded to God in worship. In Nehemiah 9, they confessed their sins to the Lord. They admitted that their hearts turned from God, in part, because they forgot His great and gracious works for them on their behalf (v. 17). After their confession, they committed in a signed vow to be faithful to the Lord in a few very specific areas: they wouldn't intermarry with others to preserve their Hebrew faith (10:30), they wouldn't profane the Sabbath with merchandise (10:31), and they would give to the work of the temple (10:33).

But the people were unable to live up to their commitments. When Nehemiah returned to Persia, as he promised, the people miserably violated each of their specific vows (Neh. 13). They were no longer valuing the work of the temple. The Levites, those who served in the temple, had to find another vocation because their needs weren't met through the giving of God's people. Work was occurring on the Sabbath again, and the people were intermarrying again, causing God's people to not know the language of Judah. The people failed in every one of their vows. They couldn't keep even one. There wasn't one glimmer of hope, not one indication that they could be faithful to the Lord.

Nehemiah begs God to remember him, and then the book ends. Just like that.

The book ends with a painful picture of our inability to follow through on our bold commitments to the Lord. We're left with the humbling realization that we can't keep our vows. We're utterly incapable, in our own merit, of delivering on our commitments. The abrupt and bitter ending is intentional. The *written* Word is shepherding us to our need for the living Word—for Jesus. What the people in the book of Nehemiah needed, and what we find in Christ, is a new covenant written on our hearts (Jer. 31:33).

The ending of the book of Nehemiah is both humbling and hopeful for leaders in God's Church. It is humbling because we understand how challenging it is to cultivate culture. It is hopeful because of Jesus. Because of God's grace, because He replaces hearts of stone with hearts of flesh, we can have great hope for our church cultures. Who better to understand transformation than the people of God who have been transformed? Can anyone better than Christ-followers understand what it means to be changed? We are transformed people.

Managing Church Culture

As leaders we do not just make big culture changes, we manage culture constantly. To manage culture, church leaders will need to influence and shape the foundational beliefs of the church community, while helping those beliefs find meaningful expression. More than just providing a picture of a future reality, culture-shaping leaders help establish the worldview necessary to bring about that future. Managing culture is an invasive, sweeping, and ongoing effort.

All too often, leaders underestimate the time and the constant pressure required for managing church culture. As a culture is forming and old worldviews are being transformed, there are adjustment periods filled with tension, trial and error, and lots of rehashing of conversations. Changing practices or strategies is one thing, but driving change while protecting and shaping culture is quite another. And changes in practice do not last if they are not used to help create a new culture and are not grounded in that culture. This challenging paradox points to the power of culture. The culture cannot be shaped easily, but it must be managed well or a new approach and vision can have unexpected effects on culture.

Managing culture in the church is not simply an act of going from one strategy to another. It's not just changing a mission statement or language to get a better result. We are not like the world who attempts to find the right set of values to maximize shareholder value or increase market share. Our desire to shape church culture is a direct action to lead the body of Christ to follow the rule of God. The worldview we are forming in our church is not an arbitrary set of altruistic values. The culture we form in our churches is the set of beliefs and behaviors of God's people as they strive by faith to obey God's Word. So, church leaders who labor to lead church culture are actually leading our churches to repent of common idols, to reject common lies, to forsake ungodly behaviors, and to embrace the lordship of Jesus over the Church.

To offer a simple model for managing culture, we will work from the following illustration:

MANAGING
CHURCH CULTURE

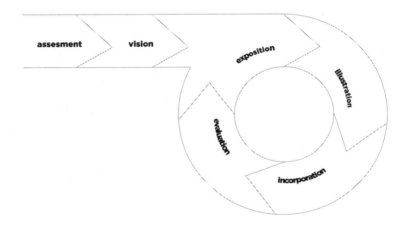

Assessment. Churches are similar to "many organizations that neither understand their current culture nor the preferred culture which would best help them achieve their goals."[8] To know if your culture is helpful in creating leaders, you must first assess. Uncover the values that are really believed by observing the behavior, by listening to the stories, by seeing what is celebrated and what is tolerated in the culture. As you assess the church culture, look for values that are affirmable. Even in a ministry culture where change is necessary, there are values that are affirmable. Identify the values beneath the surface that you want to remain, values that are excellent and praiseworthy. What values existed when the church started? What values were prevalent when the church was the healthiest?

It is unwise simply to bring a list of "aspirational" values and attempt to reverse-engineer them into the culture. Find what actual beliefs and values are affirmable and affirm, celebrate, and reinforce them. Starve and confront the unhealthy ones, but affirm the healthy actual values and the right beliefs. Leaders can bring new values into a culture, but if leaders are not lifting up actual values, they are not really leading where they are, but someplace else, some other group or church they dream about.

Vision Cast. Once the church culture is assessed, the hard work really begins. The leadership of the local church must take the next, daring step: casting a new vision for a healthy culture that makes disciples and reproduces leaders. As a vision is shared for developing leaders, the vision must be rooted in biblical conviction. The church must hear that she is on the planet to make disciples, that the mission is urgent, and that God has called His people as missionaries into all spheres of life. Changing culture is changing the fundamental narrative of a local body of believers.

Casting vision is all the more challenging when sin must be confronted. For Christians, our unwanted behaviors are often not just unhelpful or nonstrategic; often what needs to be addressed is actually sin. This makes forming culture a gut-wrenching experience. We are not simply moving people past their previous mistakes and misunderstandings. Rather, culture change through vision-casting in the local church often means walking the church through corporate repentance.

Churches, and church leaders, cannot be simple pragmatists attempting to get the most effective behaviors to produce the greatest return. Instead, we are worshippers, living under the kind rule of our Sovereign Father. The local church needs brave culture leaders. We need to paint wonderful pictures of future obedience, while leading our churches to repent of our past failures. In order to move our people into a new season of obedience, grief is an appropriate response.

This grief in Scripture is not just an individual activity; it's a corporate activity, led by church leaders. Peter preached the first gospel message with an aim of producing grief over sin. He accused them of crucifying and killing Jesus (Acts 2:23, 36). Their response? "They were cut to the heart . . . and said, 'Brothers, what must we do?'" (v. 37). They experienced grief of sin, which produced repentance (v. 38).[9] The path forward for the Christian church is through the road of repentance. The content of this vision will become a roadmap. What theological convictions need to be changed, added, or forgotten? What will it look like once the new convictions are embraced?

Careful thought here will serve the Church for years to come. Churches often find themselves disconnecting their strategic plans from their grievances with church culture. Leaders see a particular problem, but we want to move past repentance right into obedience. Leadership like this only glorifies our own wisdom and righteousness. Appropriate corporate repentance magnifies the Lord of mercy in the church. Not only this, but members of our churches see what we see. When major unbiblical deviations go unaddressed, it only serves to undermine the membership's view of the care, courage, or competency of the leadership. If we want to see something in culture change, we need to get specific.

Exposition. This next stage of managing change will begin a circular process. In this stage, new identified elements of needed cultural change will be added to the existing healthy elements of culture being maintained and reinforced. The leadership team will find itself running around the process circle from exposition to illustration to incorporation to evaluation and a back again to exposition. It may take more laps than a NASCAR race, but culture will change over time. And the process must never end because the culture must be continually cultivated.

Exposition is the step in the process that gives Christ-followers a tremendous confidence in the possible future for any church.

While formation is always challenging, who better to understand than those the Lord is sanctifying daily? Every single day, we must come to our Bible expecting God to change us, renew us, and cause us to repent. It should be no different for the Church of God. And the means that God uses to shape individuals is the same means He will use to change a church's culture. The teaching and preaching of God's Word is our hope and God's power for change. This step in culture change is so important. The Word of God is powerful to renew hearts and produce fruit among God's people.

Leaders manage and change church culture most effectively and accurately when expositing the Word of God. God can, and does, change our presuppositions, our foundational beliefs, and our very core identities. He does it all the time. In the same way, if we want to develop cultures of leadership development in the local church, we will need to be renewed by the Word of God. We should not expect that the members of our congregation have any more capacity than we do to behave differently apart from the work of the Holy Spirit through the Word of God. As we teach the text, we are utilizing God's means to conform the Church to His glorious image.

Managing culture through exposition is not simply a tool in the belt; it is the work of discipleship at the congregational level. There is a power in exposition that nothing else can match. When we lead our churches through exposition, we are leading them to grow by trusting God. What a glorious thing to join God in His work in drawing men and women to trust in Him.

Whether we are correcting belief in the culture, affirming a crucial conviction, or training for a new behavior, it is crucial for the local church to shape culture according to God's design. It will take time, but God is in the business of renewing our minds, as well as our lives. For a church to change into an epicenter of leadership development, God's Word will lead the way. Strategic visions and professional frameworks will never have the power to replace the exposition of God's Word.

Illustration. To form culture, the leader must make the exposition come alive. As people born into history, born into a specific time and a specific place, we need to be able to touch, feel, and see ideas and concepts. We learn from a very young age that people learn more by watching than by hearing. For a culture to really change, it needs new stories, new heroes, and even new villains. As leaders labor for new culture or reinforce a healthy one in a local church, there are few tasks more crucial than providing concrete examples. This can, and should, be done first by personal modeling on the part of the leader. People will follow your example before they follow your vision.

Paul, in leading change in the Corinthian church, utilizes this very tactic. After careful teaching on the proper use (and laying down of) freedoms in Christ, Paul offers himself as the model: "Imitate me, as I also imitate Christ" (1 Cor. 11:1). Our friend Tony Merida says it this way, "Let them see themselves in light of your struggle and show them the same grace that you have discovered. . . . You are not on display; the Living God is. And your goal is for others to love Him and be satisfied in Him."[10]

The leader has more tools than just modeling to help solidify new cultural narratives. One of the most powerful tools for illustration is the use of heroes and villains. In the local church we do it through testimony and appreciation of faithful volunteers. We acknowledge when someone is embracing truth and obeying Christ, and we put them on display for others to imitate. There is a danger in any hero other than Jesus. We want to spend the sweeping majority of our time and energy making much of Jesus and pointing others to Him as the ultimate Hero for all righteous living. But a church can benefit from lesser heroes who show people what repentance looks like, how developing others can happen in the midst of a regular workweek, and how one can approach work with a holy sense of mission.

If the local church is to become a force for developing new leaders, then our congregations will need to see the stories of these new leaders. If a church sees regular examples of people they know used by God as leaders, the Spirit will surely begin to stir many more to action. So many lies that lead to apathy can be struck down through the right use of story in the local church. God's people are encouraged, strengthened, and stretched when the tide of God's movement seems to be swelling around them. Far too many churches fail to tell the story of God's great power, and in doing so, fail to use testimony for its intended purpose.

Villains, on the other hand, are a seldom-utilized tool in Christian circles. We think our hesitancy in using villain stories actually comes from a good place. Still, what we find in the wisdom of Scripture is a broad use of villain stores for the shaping of the worldview for people of God. A villain story is a narrative of warning. On our best days we learn to obey God simply by "believing yet not seeing." Other days, we trust God because of His historical faithfulness in the particular area. There are some days, however, when only a warning will keep us true. Paul utilizes this to reinforce proper Christian behavior in the local church when he highlights villains such as the "party of the circumcision" (Gal. 2:12 NASB) and "men of flesh" (1 Cor. 3:1 NASB). These of course represent real people, but are also a sign to the faithful to avoid their folly. As a church seeks to develop leaders, a villain is not a particular person in your church—not someone you would name in front of the congregation—but a picture of a wasted life, of the futility of living for the temporary pleasures of today instead of embracing the mission of God.

Incorporation. We will spend the next two chapters honing in on this particular aspect of cultural formation. In the next section we will help provide the necessary constructs, or structures, to incorporate a conviction for leadership development into the culture of the local church. The process of incorporation is the creation of systems, policies, structures, the reallocation of resources, and other such things to reorient the church around its new desired cultural ambitions. To help people see the tangible expression of leadership development, they must see the systems and constructs that are employed to carry out the mission of developing leaders.

Too many times change falls flat because the teaching on the new value or behavior cannot be expressed within the current restraints of the system. Imagine if a church preached ten weeks in a row on the need to develop leaders and gave testimonies every week of powerful life change and exciting moments with God as people lived out the reality of their design to lead. But, at the end of the series, as the people were excited about learning to lead and eager to be developed, nothing was offered to them. In many churches there is no tangible opportunity to put into practice what was just declared. Do you see the problem? If developing leaders is essential, the church must incorporate the conviction into the normal rhythm of the church.

Evaluation. After all is said and done, the work is never done. The binding step of the process to manage culture is the one that also makes it flexible. In the midst of cultural formation there must be regular evaluation of the results. As we teach on correct foundational beliefs, or as we challenge new deviant behaviors, there will always be a need to reinforce, redirect, or rearticulate the theology beneath the culture.

To measure progress, a church needs to establish specific goals and outcomes. As many have learned, the wrong measurements in church ministry can lead to incomplete ministry focus at best and disastrous, even idolatrous, results at worse. For a church to take seriously the holy endeavor of developing leaders, then measuring weekend attendance and offerings is insufficient. Leaders being developed, missionaries being commissioned, pastors being set apart, and multiplying godly leaders in all spheres of life will be something that is evaluated.

When leader development becomes something the church culture embraces, all ministries in the church will be expected to equip and encourage leaders. Success in the worship ministry, the kid's ministry, and the group ministry will include leaders being developed and deployed. Development will not be relegated to a single staff member or department, but will permeate the whole church. Evaluation, of course, helps ensure this happens—that each ministry and each ministry leader embraces the blessed burden of equipping others.

Not Just an Organization

When ministry leaders consider culture, read about cultural formation, discuss change initiatives, and whiteboard change strategies, we must remember that we are not talking about just an organization. Though a local church is organized (even the disorganized ones), she is much more. She is His bride, His body, and His family. Church culture must be shaped and changed with prayerfulness, in community with other godly leaders, and with great intentionality.

Shaping culture is much more difficult than changing staff, worship style, logos, programs, or even the name of a church. And yet because people are often most attached to those lesser things, those are the changes often most feared. Culture transformation, however, will take much longer.

There is much at risk if we treat cultural change like a wind-up toy that we just let loose. "Failed attempts to change often produce cynicism, frustration, loss of trust, and deterioration in morale among organizational members."[11] A failure in this endeavor is one expensive mistake, and one that future leaders will need to overcome. So while your culture is more important than most people realize, tread carefully and prayerfully as you diagnose, change, and manage.

But you must care about your culture. Without a healthy culture that actually believes and values God's people being developed as leaders in all spheres of life, constructs and leadership development initiatives will be exhausting. They will be working against a culture that does not understand or embrace them.

You must care about culture because church culture is a theological issue. To lead God's Church cannot be an exercise in pragmatism; it must be an exercise of worship to Him.

A church can and should be a leadership locus, a center of development and deployment for men and women joining God on His mission. A strong *conviction* and a healthy *culture* are essential for a church to create and commission leaders. But *constructs* are important as well. And to constructs we now turn. . . .

Constructs

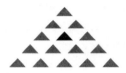

"Constructs are the systems, processes, and programs utilized to help develop leaders."

Beliefs *and* Behavior in a Culture

Thoughtful leaders know beliefs and behavior both reside within an organizational or ministry culture. Culture is continually formed as the shared beliefs and values are actually lived out in the culture. But leaders often debate which comes first, beliefs or behavior. Ralph Waldo Emerson wrote, "The ancestor of every action is a thought." On the other hand, British prime minister and contemporary of Emerson, Benjamin Disraeli, believed that "thought is the child of action."

In terms of leadership development in a church, some ministry leaders would insist on culture first. They would articulate to keep focusing on the right culture and helpful constructs will be the overflow of the culture that is being created. Others will insist that constructs are the tool to form culture.

For culture to really be sustainable, it must be formed by shared convictions. There is great danger in teaching people how to behave without their hearts being changed by continually beholding the greatness of Jesus. Just read the book of Galatians to discover the destruction of a church culture when behavior is emphasized over and apart from firm belief in the grace of God. Beliefs really do impact behavior. As the Lord renews our minds, our actions are impacted (Rom. 12:2). As the Lord transforms our hearts, we live in response to what He has done for us.

At the same time, we have seen countless ministry leaders disregard constructs as they attempt to speak a new culture into existence. Preachers preach louder and longer, and often the culture is not changed. They disregard how a construct, a tangible and visible tool, can give people a sense of what is really important. A leadership pipeline, for example, shows people "we value leadership development so much that we have a plan to make it happen."

Both culture and constructs are essential, and they must work together. If leadership development is really in the culture of a church, the culture will drive the church to have constructs. In many ways, constructs (or the lack of constructs) are the expression of your culture. At the same time, God will use development constructs to reinforce and help build a culture of leadership development. Culture and constructs must synergistically work together.

While we would side with Emerson in our belief that our beliefs and convictions must come first, we cannot disregard the power of constructs as an expression of a culture and as a tool to help form culture. On the quandary of beliefs or behavior, Robert Sutton and Huggy Rao in their book, *Scaling Up Excellence*, write, "You can target both beliefs and behavior at once. The key is creating and fueling a virtuous circle."[1] Create a virtuous cycle of culture and constructs.

CHAPTER SEVEN

DISCIPLESHIP AND LEADERSHIP DEVELOPMENT

*Jesus' concern was not with programs to
reach the multitudes, but with men whom
the multitudes would follow.*
—ROBERT COLEMAN

Often ministry leaders will ask, "What do you do for discipleship?" and then a few moments later ask, "What do you do for leadership development?"—as if the two are mutually exclusive. Jesus did not divorce leadership development from discipleship. As He invested in the Twelve, He continually "discipled" them while simultaneously developing them to be leaders. While it may be helpful to view leadership development as advanced discipleship or as a subset of discipleship, it is detrimental to view leadership development as distinct from discipleship.

The Church holds the conviction to develop others for the future. More than any organization, team, or institution, developing future leaders is in the people of God's DNA. God's people have always multiplied. The faith has always, by God's grace, been transferred from one generation to the next, from one person to another.

For Christ-followers, developing others is much more than an item on a list of five essential things one must do. It is a conviction that is deeply connected to what it means to be a Christ-follower. We are Christians because others have shared the gospel with us. We have matured because others have helped develop us. We are a part of a long and beautiful lineage, a long and beautiful history, of Christ-followers multiplying.

We have great biblical examples of leaders developing others. Joshua is first mentioned in Scripture when Moses chose him to lead the Israelite army (Exod. 17:9). Moses developed Joshua into the leader who would lead God's people into the land He gave them. The Lord commanded Elijah to train Elisha (1 Kings 19:16), and Elijah invested in Elisha before Elisha succeeded him. Paul invited Timothy to join him on the mission of spreading the gospel and challenged him to entrust the message to others the same way Paul entrusted the message to Timothy (2 Tim. 2:2). And then there is Jesus . . .

Jesus, the Discipler

Jesus, our Savior-King, was born into a rabbi/disciple culture. In His providence, He was born into a religious culture that valued development, as rabbis would invite disciples to follow and learn. When Jesus invited His disciples to follow Him, He was inviting them to become like Him, to become like their Rabbi.

The only time the Bible records Jesus praying all night was before He chose His disciples (Luke 6:12–13). He chose to ensure the gospel would spread through the disciples, and He prayerfully selected those to whom He would hand the mission. Robert Coleman masterfully wrote:

> It all started by Jesus calling a few men to follow him. His concern was not with programs to reach the multitudes, but with men, whom the multitudes would follow. Remarkable

as it may seem, Jesus started to gather these men before he ever organized an evangelistic campaign or even preached a sermon in public. Men were to be his method of winning the world to God.[1]

Jesus could have chosen any method to ensure the world would hear of His gracious sacrifice for them, to ensure that the message would be shared around the globe. The world is His, so all resources were at His disposal. He is not bound or limited by the laws of this world, so no plan could be thwarted. He is the only Creator, so He could have designed a means to communicate or broadcast His life and death to the world. He could have assembled the world to Himself, to observe His death or resurrection. He could have chosen any method imaginable or unimaginable, yet He chose discipling people who would disciple people.

From a worldly perspective, Jesus' ministry was not a huge success. His ministry began with a jeer from a disciple, "Can anything good come out of Nazareth?" (John 1:46) and ended with a lonely death. In the middle, His own brothers did not believe Him and one of His own disciples betrayed Him. From the height of His popularity, His following dwindled significantly. At one time there were five thousand men (much more with women and children) listening to His sermons and enjoying the free snacks before the service. But as He went to the cross, few supporters were there. Even after He conquered the grave and rose from the dead, only about 120 waited in Jerusalem for the Holy Spirit.

But His ministry forever changed the world. The disciples Jesus developed bore fruit, fruit that lasts forever. Just as Jesus discipled them, they poured their lives into others, and followers of Christ have been multiplying ever since.

Jesus chose to invest in a small group of disciples, to train them and to send them into the world. He chose disciples to ensure the message would spread and more disciples would be made. Jesus had no Plan B. He clearly told His disciples to "go . . . and make disciples" (Matt. 28:19).

Jesus still has no Plan B. Discipleship—developing believers who grow over a lifetime—is His method.

Consumption Is Not Discipleship

The Church was birthed in a discipleship paradigm, a culture where rabbis invested in their disciples. As the center of the Church moved from Jerusalem to Rome, the culture surrounding the center of the Church looked very different. With Jerusalem as the Church's center, the Church was surrounded by a rabbi/disciple model. With Rome as the Church's center, the Church was surrounded by a culture that valued professors dispensing information to students.

Through the Middle Ages, the Church began to look like the world, as unempowered "laity" attended religious services to consume what the "clergy" dispensed. People were not developed. Instead they were taught to consume religious services from their leaders, those designated as the ones closest to God.[2] Sadly the clergy during the Middle Ages did not understand or declare the gospel. So not only was consumption the paradigm, but the gospel was not being heralded—which would have destroyed the false dichotomy and division within the body of Christ.[3]

Consumption and discipleship are very, very different. Jesus launched the Church with discipleship, and she drifted to consumption.

By His grace, God raised up leaders who would usher in a reformation, a return to the gospel and an understanding that all of God's people are priests. All of God's people represent Him and serve Him in their spheres of life. Michael Horton stated, "One of the Reformation's key themes, of course, was the glad New Testament announcement that, in Martin Luther's words, 'the name and office of priest are common to all Christians.'"[4] Because all of God's people are priests, all of God's people must be discipled.

Just as the Church drifted from discipleship to consumption, local churches have the proclivity to drift as well. Consumption is much easier. Consumption is tempting because it is focused on the masses and provides an immediate action.

Here is an example of the drift in some churches. Over a decade ago, many pastors began to communicate messages such as, "Anyone can lead a small group," and, "If you can press play and make coffee, you can lead a small group." For some of these churches, these messages were a way to help change the perception of what it takes to be a group leader so that more people would view themselves as able to launch and lead a group. The logic among ministry leaders played out like this:

Problem: As we are growing, we don't have enough small groups to care for the new people who are coming to our worship services. And we know we need these people to be in a group or class.

Solution: We need to launch new small groups.

Problem: Yeah, but to launch new groups we need new group leaders. And some of the people in our church view leading a group as "being an expert teacher," and not very many people feel they are good teachers.

Solution: We must change the perception of what it means to be a group leader. We need a larger pool to recruit from. Let's make it easier to be a group leader.

And the "anyone can be a small group leader" language was born. The motivation behind the message was good: getting more people into groups, more people into biblical community. But unintended consequences emerged.

Group leaders became mere facilitators, not shepherds. There is some incongruent and inconsistent messaging occurring in many churches. You really can't say, "Anyone can be a small group leader," *and*, "If you want to be cared for and known in our church, get plugged into a group." Those two messages contradict one another at the most basic philosophical level. If the group leadership bar is lowered, then so should the promise of what the group can provide. Not just "anyone" can shepherd and care for a group of people. If the groups in a church are intended to provide care, accountability, and biblical community, then not just "anyone" can lead them.

A facilitator can host a session, but it takes a leader to lead people. A facilitator can ask questions from a page, but it takes a leader to care for the person too beat up from life to attempt to answer. A host can ask a question, but it takes a leader who is on board with the theology of the church to be able to guide the discussion. We need disciple-making leaders, not merely facilitators.

Groups became about consumption, not development. If all it takes to lead a group is "pressing play and making coffee," then we shouldn't be surprised if the end result is groups that merely consume information. If groups are designed to be integral in a church's disciple-making process, then groups must be more than consumption centers. The groups must understand that they are in community together, to develop one another, to care for one another, and to grow together. If the group is going to be about more than consumption, then leaders must view their role as much deeper than merely pressing play or reading a list of questions.

The quick fix of adding more groups took many people from discipleship to consumption. Unintended consequences will always emerge in the midst of a drift toward consumption.

Why We Must Disciple

Consumption is focused on the masses and for the short-term payoff. Discipleship is focused on the person for the long run, for fruit that will last.

Churches will drift without a consistent and constant conviction for discipleship, to disciple people and develop leaders. We must not settle for consumption. Though much more challenging and difficult, we must insist on discipleship. And we must view leadership development as part of discipleship, not as distinct or divorced from it. Here is why:

Discipleship is the only means. God has designed the end *and* the means. The end is people from every tribe, tongue, and nation gathered around the throne worshipping Him because they were purchased with the blood of Christ (Rev. 5:9–10). Regardless of what happens this week, what unfolds in the news, the ending has already been made clear: God is redeeming for Himself a people from all peoples.

The end was made clear in the beginning. God preached the gospel to Abraham saying, "All the nations will be blessed through you" (Gal. 3:8). God told Abraham that people from every nation would have God's righteousness credited to them. At the beginning of the Bible, we find that God is going to pursue all peoples through His chosen people, Israel. At the end of the Bible, we find that God has gathered worshippers from every people group.

In the middle of the Bible is the means, the command Jesus gave us: "*Go, therefore, and make disciples of all nations*" (Matt. 28:19, emphasis added). We live in the middle. The *means* to the glorious end is not leadership development apart from Jesus. The *means* is not leadership development divorced from discipleship. The *means* is discipleship. He has commanded us to make disciples of all nations, disciples who will obey everything He commanded.

Discipleship impacts all of life. As Christ is more fully formed in people, the totality of their lives is impacted. Those who are overwhelmed with how Christ has served them will serve others. Those in awe of God's generosity will be generous. Those who are captivated by God's mission to rescue and redeem join Him in pursuing people who are far from God. Their serving, generosity, and sense of mission impact their relationships, their approach to their careers, and their view of life. Their growth as a disciple shapes how they lead at home, in their profession, and through all of life.

Discipleship is the only way to produce leaders that serve and bless the world. If leaders are created apart from Jesus-focused discipleship, they are created without grace-motivated service, generosity, and mission.

To view discipleship as distinct from leadership development is to propose that discipleship does not impact all of one's life. If a church approaches leadership development as distinct from discipleship, the church unintentionally communicates a false dichotomy—that one's leadership can be divorced from one's faith. Being a Christian leader must not be positioned as disconnected from living a godly life in Christ Jesus.

Leadership development apart from discipleship becomes overly skill-based. If leaders are developed apart from Jesus, the emphasis is inevitably on skills and not the heart transformed through Christ. Divorcing leadership development from discipleship can leave people more skilled and less sanctified. And when competency and skill outpace character, leaders are set up for a fall. We don't serve people well if we teach them how to lead without teaching them how to follow Him. We don't serve leaders well if we develop their skills without shepherding their character.

It is difficult to say this humbly, but maturing Christ-followers make better leaders. Even authors not writing from a distinctly Christian worldview articulate this truth without realizing it. For example, in his popular books *Emotional Intelligence* and *Primal Leadership*, researcher and author Daniel Goleman builds the case that the most effective leaders are *emotionally intelligent*. More than a high IQ (intelligence quotient), great leaders have a high EQ (emotional quotient), and are able to create environments and cultures that are highly effective. Effective leaders, Goleman contends, have the ability to manage their emotions, genuinely connect with people, offer kindness and empathy, lead with joy and inspiration, and display the master skill of patience.[5] Sounds a lot like the fruit of the Spirit in the life of a believer (Gal. 5:22–23).

Yet all the pushes for integrity and all the instructions on character development from leadership gurus won't transform a leader's heart. Inevitably after these authors reveal their findings that "character matters," their challenges and their writings quickly degenerate into futile attempts to change our own hearts. We can't change our own hearts. We can't pep-talk ourselves into transformation. Only Jesus can transform our character. We must develop leaders who are consistently led and fed by Him before they attempt to lead and feed others. Charles Spurgeon wrote:

> How was Peter prepared for feeding Christ's lambs? First, by being fed himself. The Lord gave him a breakfast before giving him a commission. You cannot feed lambs, or sheep either, unless you are fed yourself. . . . I think a teacher is very unwise who does not come to hear the gospel preached and get a meal for his own soul. First be fed, and then feed. . . . I commend to you the study of instructive books, but above all I commend the study of Christ. Let Him be your library. Get near to Jesus. An hour's communion with Jesus is the best preparation for teaching either the young or the old.[6]

Leadership development apart from being a disciple of Jesus always results in skills apart from character, in performance apart from transformation.

How People Develop

If you are going to develop leaders and focus on individuals and their maturation, it is wise to understand how people mature and grow. Because leadership development is part of discipleship, let's seek understanding from how people are transformed.

After interviews with four thousand Christians on how they have matured and grown, discussions with disciple-makers and experts in the field of discipleship, Eric and others developed the *Transformational Discipleship* framework.[7] According to the research, people grow when godly *leaders* apply the *truth* of God to their hearts while they are in a teachable *posture*. Discipleship occurs when *truth, posture,* and *leaders* converge.

Truth. The Lord transforms through His truth, and His Word is truth (John 17:17). The truth of the gospel and the truth of God's Word have the power to change us and mold us into the image of His Son. The gospel not only saves us, but it also sanctifies us. Our hearts are enabled to obey the commands of Scripture (the "do's") as our hearts are continually refreshed with what Christ has done for us.

Posture. God puts us in a teachable and moldable posture to receive His truth. For example, He will use trials, spiritual disciplines, and biblical community to soften our hearts toward His truth. You have surely observed the importance of a teachable posture as you have preached or taught the same message to a group of people, and some have been impacted while some have been hardened. The message and the messenger are the same, but the posture of each person is different.

Leaders. God uses disciples to make disciples. God uses leaders to apply grace to our hearts. Each person in the body is given the opportunity to administer grace, in a variety of forms (1 Pet. 4:10).

Because development is part of discipleship, and not divorced from it, we offer the following *Development Convergence* framework to help you understand how people are developed as leaders.

Leaders are developed as **knowledge** (truth), **experiences** (posture), and **coaching** (leaders) converge. All three are essential for a leader to be developed. Knowledge is what leaders must learn and know. Experiences encompass the ongoing opportunities to serve and put knowledge into practice. Coaching occurs when a shepherding leader applies the knowledge and experience with a new leader.

DEVELOPMENT
CONVERGENCE

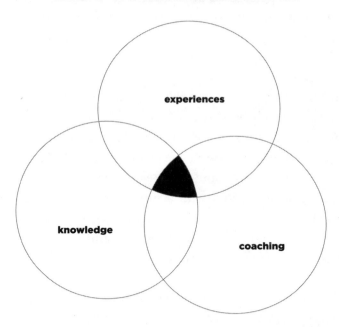

Knowledge alone will not develop a leader. Knowledge alone results in consumption and produces fat Christians with heads filled with information but hearts hardened and hands never dirty in serving others. If knowledge equated development, our churches would be filled with developed leaders as knowledge is frequently dispensed in many churches every week.

Experiences alone will not develop a leader. Experiences apart from knowledge and coaching can actually produce ineffective and unhealthy leaders who are shaped by poor experiences and unhealthy ministry environments. Without truth applied to hearts, experiences are not wisely evaluated and interpreted.

Coaching alone will not develop a leader. Without knowledge and experiences, the coach or leader has nothing to say, nothing to apply, and no feedback to give. Coaching without knowledge and experiences isn't really coaching.

The sweet spot of leadership development is the intersection of knowledge, experiences, and coaching. Scholars from a variety of fields have emphasized the convergence. For example, William Yount, Christian professor of education, articulates that effective teaching is the synergy of thinking, feeling, and doing. As thinking (knowledge), feeling (experiences), and doing (coaching) intersect, the student is spared from intellectualism without action or intellectualism without heart.[8] Ram Charan, leadership author and consultant, bemoans the lack of leadership development in organizations, even cautiously elevating it to the level of a crisis. He notes that when development does occur it is because "a senior leader takes a special interest in a junior person and provides that person with the *experiences* and *coaching* to help him or her flourish."[9] You likely recognize this intuitively and experientially. Your development occurred as knowledge was combined with coaching and experiences.

If you view development as solely informational, knowledge will be your solution. If you view development as merely behavioral, experiences will be your solution. If you view development as part of discipleship, you want to use both knowledge and experiences, alongside coaching from godly leaders, as tools for the ultimate goal of transformation.

Back to Jesus

As you read through the Gospels, you find Jesus being incredibly intentional with His disciples. While He loved the crowds, had compassion on them, and served them, the focus of His discipleship was the twelve disciples. He shared *knowledge* with them, as He often spoke directly to them, even in the midst of a crowd. He frequently and privately offered additional insights to the Twelve, explaining His teaching exclusively to them. Jesus provided *experiences* for His disciples, as He invited them to watch His interactions with people and included them in His ministry. Jesus also responded to their questions, posed questions to them, and took advantage of situations to *coach* His disciples. He applied truth to their hearts over and over again. For a detailed listing of Jesus' approach to His disciples through the lens of knowledge, experiences, and coaching, see the Appendix.

Knowledge. To develop someone, you need a base of knowledge that you are convinced must be embraced by the person being developed. According to Noel Tichey in his book *The Leadership Engine*, to develop someone, a leader must (1) take direct responsibility for the development of other leaders and (2) have teachable points they can articulate to others.[10] Which is another reason why the Church should excel in leadership development. We have a faith that has been delivered once and for all to the saints (Jude 3). We have a core set of beliefs that originated with Him, and not with us. "He gave us a new birth by the message of truth" (James 1:18), and He matures us through His truth. Unlike organizations that must develop their own core doctrine—their own core beliefs that likely shift and turn with each change in leadership—Jesus has given ours to us. His truth is timeless and transformational.

Jesus clearly held a set of beliefs that He knew the disciples must learn, so He spent a significant amount of time teaching truth to His disciples. Instead of viewing the crowd as His primary audience and the disciples as His secondary audience, Jesus flipped the paradigm. Jesus spoke to His disciples first, and the crowd overheard.

Most would think that the reasonable approach would be to address the majority of the people, but because discipleship is His method, Jesus' approach was upside-down. He focused on His disciples. The crowd was His secondary audience.

Luke 12 provides us a snapshot of Jesus' intense focus on teaching His disciples, His concern to deliver knowledge to them. A massive crowd gathered around Jesus, so much so that people were trampling on one another. And Jesus began to "say to His disciples *first*" (Luke 12:1, emphasis added). His first concern was not the crowd, but His disciples.

Try to understand the scene. Imagine showing up at a major event to hear an incredible communicator. The stadium is sold out. Christians are honking at one another in the massive parking lot and cutting in front of one another in line, vying for the best seats (yes, this actually happens). You finally sit down with your Diet Coke and chicken sandwich, ready to hear from an incredible teacher. To your surprise, he invites a small group on the stage with him and speaks to them while you are sitting in the crowd. You think, *Is this some type of illustration?* But he continues. He keeps going. Finally someone asks the speaker a question. The famous speaker answers but then turns back to the small group and continues addressing them directly. This is pretty much the scene in Luke 12.

Jesus was teaching His disciples in the midst of a huge crowd, a crowd who has been waiting for this moment—this moment to see Jesus. After someone asked questions about dividing an inheritance, Jesus answered Him with a parable and then again spoke *directly* to His disciples about not worrying, trusting God, seeking Him first, and being prepared (Luke 12:13–40). As you read the narrative, you get the sense that perhaps Peter feels badly for the crowd. He even asks Jesus, "Lord, are You telling this parable to us or to everyone?" In other words, "Jesus, there are a whole bunch of people here. Watching and listening to You right now. Are You thinking this is for them too?" Jesus didn't answer Peter. He kept speaking to His disciples about faithfulness and suffering (Luke 12:41–53).

Why did Jesus focus so passionately on giving knowledge to His disciples? He knew His time with them was short, and they were the focus of His urgency. In John 17, in His prayer in the Garden of Gethsemane for His disciples, Jesus prayed:

> "I have revealed Your name to the men You gave Me from the world. They were Yours, You gave them to Me, and they have kept Your word. Now they know that all things You have given to Me are from You, because the words that You gave Me, I have given them. They have received them . . ." (John 17:6–8)

With great intentionality, Jesus gave His disciples the knowledge they needed to receive. What a glorious picture! He left His role as disciple-maker knowing "the words that You gave Me, I have given them." A time is approaching when all leaders will vacate their roles too, including you. Wise leaders envision that day and work backward.

Experiences. To develop someone, you must provide experiences that accelerate learning and development. We often learn best by *doing*. New teachers learn as much during "student teaching" as they did the previous 3.5 years sitting in a classroom. College graduates often remark that they learned infinitely more during their internships than during their time in the classroom. You did not learn how to dribble a basketball by watching videos. Your learning accelerated when you picked up a ball. On-the-job training is the best. Experiences not only help us learn, but they reveal to us what we still need to learn. They help us long for *knowledge* and *coaching*. They help show us where we still need to grow.

Ministry experiences often put people in a teachable posture. They are given the opportunity to experience God working through them to serve others. The overwhelming moments of leading a group for the first time, attempting to connect with a group of kids or students, or engaging in a mission project can place a person in a dependent posture—where the person keenly senses the need for the Lord. Inviting someone to an overwhelming ministry experience is inviting that person into a teachable posture.

Jesus' training of His disciples happened along the way and provided them an immense amount of experiences. It was education through immersion. He invited the disciples to be with Him, to learn by watching His life. They found Him praying and saw in Him a holy dependence on the Father. They found Him talking to a Samaritan woman and learned that grace transcends cultural boundaries. They watched as He lovingly wept with Mary and Martha in their pain, and learned how to minister in the midst of grief. In their time in Jericho, they saw Jesus serve the poor (a blind man begging) and the rich (Zaccheus) and learned how to love and pursue people from different backgrounds.

In the Upper Room, the disciples watched with awe as Jesus got up from the meal, poured water into a basin, and washed their feet. Because the room where they were meeting was borrowed, a servant was not there to wash the feet of the guests. So Jesus—"assuming the form of a slave"—performed the task reserved for the lowliest slave and washed the dirty, dusty feet of His disciples, feet covered in sandals and not by shoes, feet that walked through the streets of Jerusalem during an extremely busy week. They had been arguing, again, about who was the greatest (Luke 22:24), and in the midst of their bickering Jesus showed them the full extent of His love.

Jesus also provided experiences for His disciples by involving them, by handing responsibilities to them, and by serving alongside them. Instead of baptizing people Himself, the disciples baptized.

When Jesus fed the five thousand, He involved His disciples in the miracle. They distributed the baskets and collected the leftovers. When Jesus walked on water, He invited Peter to walk on water with Him.

Jesus consistently provided experiences to prepare the Twelve, to develop them into the leaders that would influence and impact the entire world. In some moments, Jesus taught His disciples how to minister by ministering. In other moments, He more directly involved them. And in other moments, He sent them to serve without Him.

John records none of the parables in his gospel because, to John, all of Jesus' life was a parable.[11] He closed his gospel with the statement:

> And there are also many other things that Jesus did, which, if they were written one by one, I suppose not even the world itself could contain the books that would be written. (John 21:25)

The lessons were too many to record, the impact so significant that John viewed the task of writing it all down to be impossible. John and the other disciples learned by simply being with their disciple-maker, by experiencing life together.

Coaching. Jesus shared knowledge with His disciples and invited them to experience life with Him, but He also applied truth to their hearts as questions and situations arose. He asked penetrating questions, responded to theirs, and took full advantage of everyday situations to develop them.

His coaching was constant. When people began to stop following Jesus, He asked the Twelve if they were going to leave too. After calming the storm, Jesus asked the disciples: "Where is your faith?" After the disciples could not cast a demon out, Jesus emphasized that "this kind can only come out with prayer and fasting." When James and John wanted to destroy people with fire,

Jesus confronted them for their lack of love. After watching Jesus continually pray, the disciples asked Jesus to teach them. Jesus gave them an example of how to pray and challenged them to be persistent in prayer. Jesus corrected His disciples for stopping children from coming to Him, and used the moment to remind them of childlike faith.

Luke's gospel provides us a sense of how Jesus moved His disciples from merely watching Him serve others to coaching His disciples in their ministry to others.[12] We see a rhythm of "watch, go, and let's talk." After the Twelve were designated as His disciples (Luke 6:13), they first watched Him minister. They were then sent out to minister before coming back to Jesus to discuss what happened on their journey.

Watch (Luke 7–8). At first, Jesus invited His disciples to simply be with Him. His presence was the essence of their development. They saw His focus, His love, and His mercy and compassion toward people for ministry. They saw Jesus receive worship from a sinful woman and defend her before the religious. They observed as He mercifully drew attention to a woman who was healed from her bleeding, so that all would know she was no longer unclean. They saw Him relate to a family in the midst of grief and pain before raising their daughter from the dead.

Go (Luke 9–10). After the disciples watched Jesus serve, Jesus sent them to minister to others and proclaim the Kingdom of God. Twice in Luke 9 and 10, Jesus sent the disciples and others to minister. He gave them specific instructions on how to respond to people who were hospitable, how to respond to those who were not welcoming, and what to take for the journey.

Let's talk (Luke 9–10). In both instances, when the disciples returned from serving and proclaiming, they shared their experiences with Him. Essentially, they debriefed. They were thrilled with the impact they were having. They were enjoying the serving buzz, the joy that comes from seeing lives transformed. As they rejoiced in the fruit of their ministry, Jesus challenged them to rejoice that their names are written in heaven—to rejoice first in the reality that they are His. In other words, the coaching Jesus provided focused on their hearts. He wanted them to be more in awe of what the Lord had done for them than what He was doing through them.

Leadership Development Imperatives

If you and your church are going to develop leaders, you must deliver knowledge, provide experiences, and offer coaching. As people receive truth from godly leaders they trust and respect while they are in a serving posture, development is likely to occur.

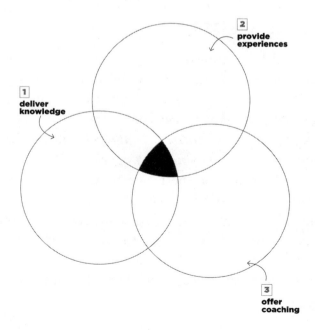

LEADER DEVELOPMENT
IMPERATIVES

2
provide
experiences

1
deliver
knowledge

3
offer
coaching

1. Deliver Knowledge

Knowledge includes information, but it is much more than knowing facts or being able to understand and sign off on a doctrinal statement. To *know* a friend or spouse is to know much more than their favorite color or restaurant; it is to recognize their moods, to know how to encourage, and to be skilled in relating to them. To *know* something is to understand it well, to be skilled in it. So when a church delivers knowledge to leaders they are developing, the church is delivering knowledge to more than just the mind.

When the apostle Peter preached the sermon that launched the church in Jerusalem, those listening were impacted in head, heart, and hands. All three domains were involved.[13]

> "Therefore let all the house of Israel know with certainty that God has made this Jesus, whom you crucified, both Lord and Messiah!" When they heard this *[head]*, they came under deep conviction *[heart]* and said to Peter and the rest of the apostles: "Brothers, what must we do?" *[hands]* (Acts 2:36–37)

Head: To deliver knowledge to the minds of leaders you are seeking to develop, you must know what you believe they must know. In other words, you must have an established sphere of knowledge that you want to pass on to those you are developing. Some questions to consider are: *What do leaders need to know? What competencies do they need to develop?*

We wanted to answer these questions, so we gathered with ministry leaders who are passionate about and committed to developing others. We sought to develop a simple set of competencies that transcend ministry context and ministry role—a set of competencies that we believe leaders must learn. From our time in the Scripture and our combined experiences learning from effective leaders, we distilled the competencies to the following six, which we will further discuss in the next chapter:

- Discipleship: theological and spiritual development
- Vision: preferred future
- Strategy: plan or method for the preferred future
- Collaboration: ability to work with others
- People development: contributing to the growth of others
- Stewardship: overseeing resources within one's care

Heart: As we apply knowledge, we must apply knowledge to the hearts of those we are developing. Heads filled with information without hearts transformed by the grace of God is a horrific combination in the realm of leadership development. As King Saul continued ruling, surely his head was filled with more and more knowledge of how to direct people and administer his kingdom. But his heart wandered more and more from the One who ultimately made him king.

As Saul's leadership and responsibility increased, the cracks in his character became more visible and pronounced. His heart could not handle others developing and growing. He was filled with jealousy as songs were sung, "Saul has killed his thousands, but David his tens of thousands" (1 Sam. 18:7). His heart could not handle victory, either. After defeating the Amalekites, in pride Saul disobeyed the Lord's command and instead built a monument to himself (1 Sam. 15:12). Both pain and victory exposed Saul's character. Pride, jealousy, and fits of anger raged within his heart. Saul's ability to lead outpaced his character. His skills were greater than his integrity. And the Lord regretted that He had made Saul king (1 Sam. 15:11). Greater responsibility tends to reveal one's character. We must deliver knowledge to the hearts of those being developed, not just the heads.

Hands: As leaders are developed in their thinking and in their affections, they must also be equipped with knowledge to serve.

They must be taught how to lead, how to serve. Zeal for leading, without knowledge of how to lead is not good (Prov. 19:2). Zeal without knowledge is dangerous because we can be deeply and sincerely passionate and completely misguided.[14] As competencies are taught, wise leaders connect these competencies to actions.

2. Provide Experiences

Each week ministry leaders feel the weight of responsibility to disciple people in the church while also owning the responsibility of "pulling off church" that week. The kids' ministry, student program, weekend services, and mission activity won't happen without the help of others, without volunteers engaged in the ministry. Sometimes these two responsibilities are viewed as polarizing opposites, as if ministry leaders are confronted with the choice to either (a) disciple someone, or (b) invite a person to serve. The dichotomy is unnecessary and unhelpful as people can and should be developed *through* ministry experiences.

Church leaders must confidently invite people to serve, knowing that the opportunities to serve provide moments where development occurs. Churches must emphasize that all of God's people are ministers and have the opportunity to influence and impact others through the ministry of the Church.

Some questions to consider are: *Is it easy for someone to find a serving opportunity at our church? Is there a culture of inviting, where current leaders are encouraged to invite others to serve alongside them?*

3. Offer Coaching

In his book *Talent Is Overrated*, Geoff Colvin makes the strong case that the top performers in any field have engaged in "deliberate practice" for sustained seasons of their lives. The practice is "designed to improve performance, often with a teacher's help," and "the practice activity provides feedback on a continual basis."[15] Those who hone their craft have been fortunate to have people throughout their lives provide real-time feedback. Coaching from someone we trust and respect deeply impacts our development.

Ministry experiences present many teachable moments, and when those moments are shepherded by a godly leader, development increases. A godly leader applying the truth of God to the heart must converge with the teachable posture that serving provides. Development and discipleship are relational, not merely informational. Without the truth applied to hearts, all a church produces is people who accomplish tasks.

As Jesus cared for the hearts of His disciples when they excitedly returned from ministering, so, too, a church must care for the hearts and not just the actions. As Jesus reminded the disciples that they were forgiven sons first, so, too, must church leaders remind those being developed of their fundamental identity. If leaders are not constantly reminding people of Jesus and His grace, development will degenerate into altruistic legalism—attempts to justify oneself through deeds that are applauded and boost one's self-image.

Remind people that they are serving because He has first served us, not because we are attempting to earn His love or pay Him back for His love. There is nothing to be paid back as the debt has been paid in full. If you lead a team in the hospitality ministry, remind them that Christ first welcomed us. If you lead a team in the worship ministry, remind them of the joy of celebrating who He is and what He has done for us through Christ. If you lead a team in the kids' ministry, remind them God's Kingdom is ultimately for children, for those of us who trust Him as our Father.

Some questions to consider are: *Do we have conversations with those serving in our church about their experiences and about what the Lord is teaching them? Are we constantly reminding people of the "why" beneath the serving?*

Leaders are responsible for future leaders. Development is part of discipleship. To develop other leaders, deliver knowledge, provide experiences, and offer coaching.

PIPELINES AND PATHWAYS

Leaders aren't born, they are made. And they are
made just like anything else, through hard work.
—VINCE LOMBARDI

Would an effective middle school principal be a great leader in another setting? Would a basketball coach who displays leadership prowess excel in managing a local restaurant or leading a sales team? Would a great student ministry pastor make a great senior pastor? In other words, how much of leadership is transferable from one context to another, from one discipline to another discipline?

The authors of *The Leadership Code* sought to answer that question through qualitative research and interviews with well-respected leaders, and concluded that 60 to 70 percent of all leadership is applicable to any domain or context.[1]

We have argued that the Church must develop leaders for all spheres of life. If up to 70 percent of leadership is completely transferable to any domain, as churches develop leaders they are developing leaders that may effectively lead and serve in a variety of contexts. As leaders are developed in the Church, they are simultaneously developed for all spheres of life, to be men and women who represent our King and steward responsibilities and opportunities for His glory and on His mission.

The authors and researchers behind *The Leadership Code* also sought to capture the essence of the 60 to 70 percent transferable aspects of leadership, so they distilled leadership down to five essential and transferable traits: strategist, executioner, talent manager, human capital developer, and personal proficiency. Personal proficiency is what we would call integrity, being a man or woman of character.

In the illustration below, notice that the right side of the illustration is focused on the organization and the left side is focused on individuals. The top half of the chart is focused on the long-term, and the bottom-half is focused on the short-term.

THE LEADERSHIP
CODE

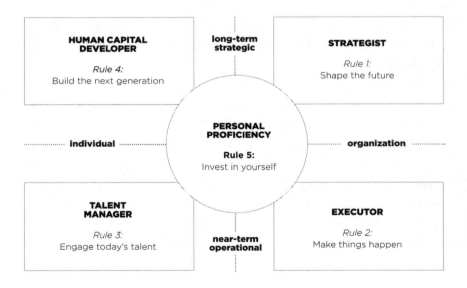

The *human capital developer* leadership trait focuses on individuals for the future. With all of leadership distilled down to five essential leadership qualities, the researchers/authors concluded that developing others, developing leaders for the future, is absolutely essential. In other words, embedded in what it means to be a leader is the responsibility to make other leaders. In all our consultations with leaders, from CEOs of for-profit companies to leaders of nonprofit organizations to pastors and ministry leaders, many have admitted that *human capital developer* is the trait, the box, they most struggle with. And for understandable reasons. The urgency of today pushes many leaders to live in "execution" and "talent manager" mode. Even as you read this, there are e-mails filling in-boxes, meeting requests being submitted, and fires burning that you sense responsibility to put out. You are always pulled down to the short-term, to the now.

Leadership development does not provide instant gratification. It does not produce immediate results. Unlike executing a plan, running a program, completing a task, or knocking out a short-term goal, developing leaders is long and hard work. It takes great discipline to develop leaders for the future. And that discipline can only come from a deeply held conviction that "a critical part of my role is to develop others." It can only come from an overwhelming sense of responsibility that "leaders are responsible for future leadership."[2]

Leadership development, with God's global mission in mind, requires the church to have an intentional plan to develop leaders. The scope of God's mission demands leadership multiplication. Because the short-term and the immediate needs will always pull you away from developing leaders, an intentional process is essential. For church leaders to be "human capital developers" who create leaders who, in turn, will develop others requires a consistent and systematic approach to leadership development. Without a systematic approach to developing and deploying leaders, churches look like cruises to nowhere.

Church Cruises to Nowhere

Several cruise lines offer cruises to *nowhere*. If you want to plan a trip to nowhere, it is really quite easy. You purchase a ticket, pack your bags for no real destination, do absolutely no research on countries or cities you will visit because you won't actually be visiting any countries or cities, plan no excursions, board a boat in Norfolk or Fort Lauderdale, and cruise to nowhere. You live on a boat for a few days and then return home having seen no real sights and gone absolutely nowhere. For relaxing and unwinding, a cruise to nowhere does have a certain appeal. Because there is no way to accomplish anything or do anything at all, some must find it relaxing.

Many churches approach leadership development like cruises to nowhere. A group of people on the same boat, in the same church, and there is nowhere in particular they are going. How can you spot a church that is like a cruise to nowhere? There is no vision and no plan for the journey.

There is no vision for the journey. On cruises to nowhere, there is not a vision for the journey. The journey is designed to take you absolutely nowhere. This must not be in the Church of Jesus Christ. A church should paint a picture of what development looks like. She should give people a vision for the journey, a view of how development occurs in the Church. Instead of leading a church to wander aimlessly in a plethora of directions, wise church leaders define and describe a journey of discipleship for the people they serve.

While sanctification—our becoming more and more like Christ—is a lifelong journey, the journey does not need to be unintentional and haphazard. Though we will not arrive at our destination of fully formed Christlikeness in this lifetime, we should be moving toward Christlikeness. And, as we do this, we call God's people to embrace the vision and conviction that they have been designed to lead. We should not be wandering aimlessly.

There is not a plan for the journey. Unlike a cruise to nowhere, a traditional cruise provides a plan and path for the people onboard. There is a plan in place that lets you know when you will arrive in each port. You know what city, what destination, is next on your journey. The ports along the way serve as markers along the journey.

A local church must do more than define discipleship and leadership development with broad, visionary language. She must also provide steps or opportunities for people to mature and develop as leaders.

Sadly, in many churches there is no plan. In every church research study I (Eric) have been involved with, the lack of intentionality in most churches has been painfully obvious. In *Simple Church,* we found that most churches have no process of discipling people. In *Transformational Groups,* we discovered that most church leaders could not articulate how groups fit into their overall strategy. And in research that undergirds this book, we learned that fewer than 25 percent of church leaders say they have a plan to develop leaders—though they know they should have one.[3]

Moving from Nowhere to Somewhere

Discipling people and developing leaders does not need to feel like a journey to nowhere. The apostle Paul's approach was very different. As he wrote about his ministry, he articulated both a vision for the journey and intentionality in developing others. Notice these two passages:

> We proclaim Him, warning and teaching everyone with all wisdom, so that we may present everyone mature in Christ.

I labor for this, striving with His strength that works powerfully in me. (Col. 1:28–29)

According to God's grace that was given to me, I have laid a foundation as a skilled master builder, and another builds on it. But each one must be careful how he builds on it. (1 Cor. 3:10)

Paul wanted to see maturity and development occur in the people he led, and this involved *teaching with wisdom*. The antithesis of teaching with wisdom is a haphazard plan or no plan for development. With similar images of intentionality, Paul described his ministry engagement as *a skilled master builder* in response to and empowered by God's grace. A wise builder has a set of blueprints, a plan, and a clear strategy for proactively attacking the building project. Building skillfully surely means more than a random and disconnected flurry of events, activities, and programs. In other words, the apostle Paul did not just "wing it" or "go with the flow." He did not haphazardly plant churches, disciple people, or develop leaders.

In this chapter we are going to provide you with tools, constructs, to help you develop leaders along the journey. The tools, we hope, will provide both a macro picture of development and also steps along the journey. But if you are here in this chapter and you have not wrestled with your own conviction for development and the culture within your church, we suggest you put the book down. If you have skipped to this chapter because this is really why you bought the book—you want some charts and graphs to make your own, pass out to your people, and declare leadership development into existence—you are doing it wrong. Without conviction for development expressed in a healthy culture, these constructs won't be of much value.

While some have the tendency to skip to this chapter, there are others who don't like the idea of constructs or systems, except when they read their *systematic* theology textbook. After all, *systems* sound so unspiritual, right? Why do we need systems when we have the Spirit? Why do we want constructs when we have Christ? We are a church not an organization! While we must be careful that our constructs are simply guides that serve and not gods that rule, the Lord has often chosen to establish and work through systems.

Case for Constructs

God is not bound by any system and no system can contain all He is, but He has chosen to use systems. God created the world out of nothing, but He did so in an orderly and systematic way. When God chose to flood the earth, He warned Noah and gave detailed instructions on how to build the ark. He gave Moses extremely specific instructions on constructing the tabernacle and designed an elaborate sacrificial system to teach His people to loathe sin and long for a once-and-for-all Sacrifice. When the Lord used Nehemiah to rebuild the wall of Jerusalem, Nehemiah strategically and systematically approached the project. In the New Testament, the apostle Paul encouraged the Corinthian believers that their gatherings should "be done in a fitting and orderly way" (1 Cor. 14:40 NIV). And God has established roles and order in the Trinity, the family, the angelic world, and the Church.

Quite simply, systems are not unspiritual. Constructs are not unholy. The God who is not bound by any system has chosen to work in a systematic fashion. You are reading this book as blood is flowing through your body because of the *circulatory system* God knit together in your body. And you are still alive for this sentence because the earth is held the precisely perfect distance from the sun in the *solar system* that God designed. While systems are important in the universe and in your body, they are also important in your church's culture. Your systems, or lack thereof, reveal your culture and help create your culture.

Systems reveal your culture. Van Halen was notorious for their "rider," a list of requests and demands artists expect from a venue. Their rider specified that a bowl of M&Ms, with the brown ones hand-removed, be placed in their dressing room before a concert. While their rider aided in building the prima-donna renown of Van Halen, it was actually a savvy system to check the culture of the venue. During that time, bands typically traveled with three semi-trucks to handle all their stage gear. Van Halen, however, traveled with *nine* semi-trucks, and their management company was concerned that venues would be unprepared to handle the weight and electrical requirements.

For safety reasons, Van Halen needed a way to know for sure that the venue had properly prepared to handle the excess load. So to determine if the venue possessed a culture of preparation, they added the statement about M&Ms to the end of their rider. If they walked into their dressing room before a show and noticed brown M&Ms in the bowl, they would immediately ask for a check on other more important requests. They often learned that the brown M&Ms was a snapshot into the overall culture of the venue, a venue that was not ready. The lack of system revealed the culture.[4]

You can tell what is important to a church by looking at their systems. If a value is strongly embedded in the culture, a system is in place to ensure the value is lived out and not merely words on a vision document. If "it" is important, a system has been designed or implemented to ensure "it" happens, whatever "it" is. For example, if caring for guests is really in the culture, there is a system in place because if pursuing guests is a deeply held cultural value in the church, then the leaders would insist on a system to ensure guests are pursued. If engaging people in ministry is in the culture, there is a system in place to deploy people into ministry. If discipling new believers is really a value, there is a system in place.

You can tell what is important to a church by looking at their systems. Conversely, you can tell what is not important to a church—no matter what the messages are—by looking at the lack of systems. What many leaders say is in the culture and believe is in the culture is not really in the culture. What many assume is happening in their churches is not. The lack of a system reveals the value is not really embedded. *Without a system, all you have is wishful thinking.*

If developing leaders is a conviction, then that conviction will drive you to a construct. The presence of a construct to help your church develop leaders, not just sign up volunteers, reveals development is important. The absence of a system reveals the conviction has not overwhelmed you to action.

Systems help create culture. Surgeon and Harvard medical professor Atul Gawande advocates for the implementation of simple checklists to help create and reinforce culture. His book *The Checklist Manifesto* chronicles research where he introduced simple checklists in eight hospitals around the world and saw tremendous results in lowering post-operation infection rates. The hospitals were in different cultural settings with different doctors, but the advent of a simple checklist system had big results.

Many church leaders have argued against their need for a system. The argument sounds like this: "All the people are different. And I am a trained pastor, one who has studied church and theology for decades. I am not one who needs a system." Gawande essentially heard the same argument from the medical community. At first medical professionals were offended or dismissive of the checklist idea. After all, each patient is different. And they were highly trained, highly educated professionals who viewed themselves above checklists.

Gawande argued that it is precisely because each patient (person) is different that a simple system is necessary, so that the baseline essentials are covered with precision every time. And the more educated and experienced the doctor (church leader) is, the more necessary a system is because of the human tendency to skip over things that are viewed as elementary. When the hospitals got on board and implemented simple systems, simple checklists, people were better served and a greater culture of safety was created.[5]

Andy Stanley, pastor of North Point Community Church in the Atlanta area, has taught that systems trump environments and ultimately change people's behavior.[6] Systems are powerful in helping to create a culture, and they assuredly reinforce the culture that exists.

If you possess a conviction for leadership development, then well-designed systems can help you create a culture that values leadership development. If you hold a deep conviction to equip people and develop leaders, the conviction will drive you to constructs, and constructs will help you create a culture that values development. Two constructs you need are the leadership pipeline and the leadership pathway. The pipeline focuses on the flock as a whole. The pathway focuses on an individual in the flock, a sheep.

Leadership Pipeline

To develop leaders on a broad scale, organizational theorists have advocated for leadership pipelines. A leadership pipeline is a helpful construct that aids in systematically and intentionally developing leaders. For example, Ram Charan, in *The Leadership Pipeline,* emphasizes the importance of developing leaders and not just hiring them. He articulates six leadership passages along the journey of development, passages that leaders must experience to be fully developed:

1. From managing self to managing others
2. From managing others to managing managers
3. From managing managers to functional manager
4. From functional manager to business manager
5. From business manager to group manager
6. From group manager to enterprise manager[7]

Though the levels of leadership in Charan's model don't translate well to local church nomenclature and practice, the thinking beneath the surface is important. Unlike the cruise to nowhere, a leadership pipeline provides both a vision for development and a process for the journey. A pipeline in the realm of local church ministry may look something like this:

lead self
(be in a group) ➡ **lead others**
(lead a group) ➡ **lead leaders**
(shepherd group leaders) ➡ **lead ministries**
(direct a ministry)

- Lead Yourself (be in a group)
- Lead Others (lead a group or team)
- Lead Leaders (shepherd or coach a group of leaders)
- Lead Ministries (direct a ministry area)

As one has proven faithful in following Christ and leading self, the person is asked to lead others. As the person proves faithful in this responsibility, the person is given the responsibility to lead and shepherd other leaders. As the person has effectively cared for and developed other leaders, the person may be willing and ready to direct a larger portion of ministry.

Our friend Dave Ferguson, pastor of Community Christian Church, articulates the leadership pipeline at his church this way:

- Apprentice Leader (leader in training)
- Leader (of ten people)
- Coach (leader of up to five leaders)
- Staff (leader of up to ten coaches)
- Campus Pastor/Church Planter (leader of staff)

Dave's pipeline focuses heavily on developing campus pastors and church planters because of the multiplying focus of Community Christian. Dave and Community Christian were on the front edge of the multiple-campus approach to multiplying, and

Dave believes that the biggest mistake multisite churches make is in failing to focus adequately on leadership development.[8] We would recommend a pipeline that serves to equip leaders for inside and outside the formed structures of the local church. Nonetheless we find the example very helpful. Regardless of the context, a leadership pipeline provides multiple benefits.

Development clarity. A pipeline provides clarity of how an organization builds its own leaders, instead of just attempting to buy them. For a ministry, a leadership pipeline is a visible picture of how leaders can be developed and what their next step in the pipeline is. The pipeline helps provide actionable understanding to the team. If you do not have a leadership pipeline, most likely people in the church are unclear about what their next step in development is.

Succession planning. A pipeline helps with succession in all roles, as leaders are being developed at all levels. When a role is open, whether staff or volunteer, a leadership pipeline helps ensure there are others ready to move into that role. Instead of reactively scrambling to "fill a spot," a leadership pipeline helps leaders think proactively about the future. If you do not have a leadership pipeline, you are likely approaching leaders from a reactive posture rather than a proactive one.

Effective coaching. As mentioned in the last chapter, the sweet spot of development is the convergence of knowledge, experience, and coaching. A pipeline helps the coaching conversations focus on development for the future and not only the role someone is currently serving in. As levels of leadership are identified, so are the character and skill-based competencies associated with those roles. Thus coaching can be directed around the necessary competencies for future roles.

Ministry expansion. As more leaders are developed, the influence of the ministry is exponentially expanded. Ministry is greatly multiplied when leaders are developed and deployed. As the scope of leadership broadens, so does the scope of ministry. The book of

Acts recounts the glorious story of God birthing and multiplying His Church. At first the growth of the Church was by addition:

> The Lord *added* to them those who were being saved. (Acts 2:47, emphasis added)

But as the Church continued her faithful witness, the growth moved from addition to multiplication.

> In those days . . . the number of disciples was *multiplying.* (Acts 6:1, emphasis added)

At this point, the growth of the Church presented new sets of challenges. The growth of a church always does. To solve the problem of some widows being underserved while also remaining focused on preaching the Word and prayer, the apostles asked the Church to select seven men, men of character and filled with the Spirit, who would serve the body. The proposal pleased the gathering of believers, they chose seven, and notice the results:

> So the preaching about God flourished, the number of the disciples in Jerusalem *multiplied greatly*, and a large group of priests became obedient to the faith. (Acts 6:7, emphasis added)

Preaching flourished. Priests were being converted. And the number of disciples multiplied greatly. In the early Church, the result of adding leaders was greater multiplication. The early Church moved from addition to multiplication to rapid multiplication as ministry responsibilities were expanded from the apostles to others. To multiply ministry and develop leaders—leaders who are "of good reputation, full of the Spirit and wisdom" (Acts 6:3)—a leadership pipeline helps people in the congregation see how the leadership base of the church may be expanded. Moreover, a leadership pipeline that develops leaders for the Kingdom can reinforce the vision that believers can lead and minister for God's glory in every context God has placed them.

Build a Pipeline

Developing and implementing a leadership pipeline is not as overwhelming as it sounds. It really takes two disciplines: intentionality and intensity. You must intentionally think about how your church or ministry will develop leaders, and you must continue down that path with great intensity, intensity expressed in persistence and not just being loud. Building a pipeline is not easy. If it were easy, churches would be excelling in developing leaders. But many are not. It takes a deep-seated conviction that will keep your intensity for development burning.

We gathered a team of seasoned church leaders—leaders who are known for developing other leaders—to discuss leadership pipeline. The goal was to walk away from gathering for several days with a template for a leadership pipeline, a view of what a leadership pipeline could be for a church—with the understanding that local churches may want to tweak and adjust for their contexts. Below were the conclusions. The first template is for a church. The second template is an example of a leadership pipeline for developing leaders who will lead and cultivate culture in environments outside the local church.

CHURCH LEADERSHIP DEVELOPMENT

pipeline level	leadership responsibilities	sample roles	discipleship	vision	strategy	collaboration	people development	stewardship	ministry-specific competencies
						core competencies			
senior leadership	Provides vision and sets the strategic direction for the church as a whole	Pastor, Executive Team, Deacon, Elder, Board Member	Teaches theology and serves as a Christ-like example	Creates vision for the church	Thinks strategically about the church as a whole	Works through team leaders	Creates a development culture	Faithfully stewards opportunities with church's resources	Ministry-specific competencies vary based on role and ministry area. These competencies progress from task execution to people development to systems management and strategy to church and ministry oversight.
ministry director	Oversees a ministry area with the responsibility of leading coaches and leaders	Children's Minister, Worship Pastor, Student Pastor	Understands and applies systematic and biblical theology and teaches spiritual disciplines	Contextualizes vision for ministry area	Designs ministry strategy and implements in ministry context	Works through leaders	Creates a development pathway for ministry area	Faithfully stewards church's resources	
leader	Provides leadership for a ministry team	Small Group Leader, Committee Chair, Teacher	Knows basic doctrines, practices spiritual disciplines, and exhibits the fruit of the Spirit	Articulates and implements vision for the ministry area	Leads others to unite around and execute ministry strategy	Works through others	Develops others	Faithfully stewards giftedness of others	
volunteer	Serves on a ministry team	Usher, Greeter, Nursery Worker	Knows the gospel and takes responsibility for personal development	Supports the vision of ministry area	Serves effectively in ministry role	Works with others	Displays willingness to be developed	Faithfully stewards personal giftedness	

PIPELINE FOR EXTERNAL LEADERS

pipeline level	leadership responsibilities	sample roles	core competencies						industry specific competencies
			discipleship	vision	strategy	collaboration	people development	stewardship	
senior/ executive leader	Provides vision and sets the strategic direction for the organization	[1] C-level officer [2] Executive Director [3] Senior Elected Official/Chief of Staff	Shapes corporate expression of the gospel for the organization and culture of the organization	Creates vision for the gospel in a particular arena	Identifies problems in an organization and develops a plan to solve, implement, and measure results	Works through key leaders	Creates a development culture	Bears responsibility for allocation of resource in alignment with biblical theology	Sector- and industry-specific competencies
director	Oversees a department with responsibility of leading managers	[1] Dir of Operations/ Marketing [2] Dir of Development [3] Policy Dir, Comm Dir	Influences corporate expression of the gospel through values and culture of a department	Contextualizes the vision of the gospel in a particular arena	Helps to identify problems and measures tasks in a department	Works through teams	Creates a development pathway for a department	Stewards department resources in alignment with biblical theology	Normally they progress from task execution to people development to systems management to organizational oversight.
team manager	Leads team members and contributes individually	[1] Functional Manager [2] Program Manager/ Supervisor [3] Functional Manager	Knows basic doctrines, practices spiritual disciplines, and begins to see the workplace as an area for expression of the gospel in demonstration and declaration	Implements the vision for the team through a gospel narrative/ biblical theology	Organizes and prepares tasks in area of assignment	Works through others	Develops others	Faithfully stewards giftedness of others and self and personal resources	
team member	Leads self, working with skill associate, or professional (contributes individually)	All staff, analyst, associate, or professional	Knows the gospel (with an emphasis on gospel narrative/biblical theology of work) and takes responsibility for personal development	Supports the vision of dept in alignment with a gospel narrative/ biblical theology	Completes tasks in area of assignment	Works with others	Displays willingness to be developed	Faithfully stewards personal giftedness and resources	

[1] **Corporation**
[2] **Non-Governmental Organization**
[3] **Government**

The previous pages are views of fully developed pipelines. To get there takes some work. Based on our work with churches and organizations, here are four critical steps:

1. Diagnose: Survey the Area

Before an engineer even considers digging and putting steel in the ground, the engineer carefully evaluates the land. You must do the same. Look at your current ministry and evaluate the leadership. How many levels of leadership currently exist in your context?

In reality your church may have a network of pipelines, depending on the size of the church. So identify levels of leadership within each ministry department. You may have one for kids' ministry leadership, one for mission leadership, one for community/groups leadership, etc. It will be helpful, however, to develop a common nomenclature for all areas in your church. But for now, identify the levels of leadership.

> How many levels of leadership do you currently have in your church?
>
> What language is used to describe each level?
>
> Could a consistent language be easily developed?
>
> What are the types of roles?

2. Design: Draw the Plans

After surveying the area, it is time to draw the plans for the leadership pipeline. The planning is critical. The design will impact how leaders are developed and the journey that is set before them. Because you will execute what you design, design carefully and prayerfully. Involve a team of people in this process. The cliché is true here: Measure twice and cut once.

Identify competencies. We are using "competencies" as the overarching term so that the pipeline can be as simple to read and absorb as possible. There are character-based competencies, such as being a disciple of Jesus, and skill-based competencies, such as developing strategy. Without competencies, a leadership pipeline is incomplete because you will be simply moving people to new roles without understanding the competencies required in those roles and the competencies that must be mastered before one moves to a new place in the leadership pipeline.

The majority of our time was developing a leadership pipeline template with the team of leaders focused on competencies. We landed on the premise that leadership development is essentially advanced discipleship, so we did not develop two different sets of competencies: one for being a disciple and one for being a leader.

The team analyzed all their collective experience of developing leaders in the church and concluded the following seven competencies are absolutely essential. Remember, earlier in this chapter we shared that research indicates 70 percent of all leadership is fully transferable from one context to another. So if a church seeks to develop leaders for the world, these competencies transfer to leaders serving in multiple spheres of life. We are offering these as an example, knowing that you may want to create your own or contextualize these:

Discipleship: *Theological and spiritual development*

Vision: *A preferred future*

Strategy: *Plan or method for the preferred future*

Collaboration: *Ability to work with others*

People Development: *Contributing to the growth of others*

Stewardship: *Overseeing resources within one's care*

Ministry Specific Competencies: *Unique skills within a ministry area*

Apply competencies to each level of leadership. After competencies have been developed, those competencies must be applied to each level of leadership. By design, someone who is at an early stage in the pipeline may not display the same level of aptitude in a competency as someone who is at an earlier stage in development.

For example, collaboration—the ability to work with others—is a critical competency for all leaders. Because leadership is about serving people, one who cannot relate to and work with others will be doomed to ineffectiveness. But the competency of collaboration will be expressed differently as leaders progress through the pipeline. And this must be the case, as the expectation for collaboration will rise as leaders have greater responsibilities. Here is an example of how a competency, like collaboration, can be applied to each level of leadership:

- Level 1: Volunteer: Works with others
- Level 2: Leader: Works through others
- Level 3: Director: Works through teams
- Level 4: Senior leadership: Works through key leaders

As leaders progress through the pipeline, they don't lose the competencies they previously developed. The leadership pipeline helps them add to what was already developed. In other words, someone does not graduate from working well with others, but the leader adds to that skill as the leader progresses through the pipeline.

Develop training plans for each competency and level of leadership. For each level of leadership in the pipeline, flesh out what training a leader will receive, what experiences will help form the leader, and what coaching will take place. On the next page is a sample training path for the "strategy competency."

STRATEGY COMPETENCY

pipeline level	leadership responsibilities	sample roles	strategy	core competencies — development outcomes
senior leadership	Provides vision and sets the strategic direction for the church as a whole	Pastor, Executive Team, Deacon, Elder, Board Member	Thinks strategically about the church as a whole	Strategy modules will equip senior leadership to: - Understand church strategy as a whole - Know the essentials of a simple strategy - Think strategically about the church's discipleship process - Evaluate existing programs and processes - Recognize and overcome strategic entropy
ministry director	Oversees a ministry area with the responsibility of leading coaches and leaders	Children's Minister, Worship Pastor, Student Pastor	Designs ministry strategy and implements in ministry context	Strategy modules will equip a ministry director to: - Design a ministry strategy - Avoid common mistakes in developing a ministry strategy - Use programs as tools in the church's discipleship process - Recognize ministry idols that disrupt focus from church's mission
leader	Provides leadership for a ministry team	Small Group Leader, Committee Chair, Teacher	Leads others to unite around and execute ministry strategy	Strategy modules will equip a leader to: - Recognize and address strategic drifts - Align a team to a ministry strategy - Communicate a ministry strategy effectively
volunteer	Serves on a ministry team	Usher, Greeter, Nursery Worker	Serves effectively in ministry role	Strategy modules will equip a volunteer to: - Understand their role within the larger context of the church's strategy - Serve effectively in ministry area

Training plans can help facilitate coaching conversations between leaders and those they are developing. Embedded in effective coaching is the important leadership discipline of providing feedback. Most churches struggle with providing feedback, under the guise of being kind and gentle. But not providing feedback is cruel. It is the kisses of the enemy that are excessive, and the wounds of a friend that are trustworthy (Prov. 27:5–6). It is loving to provide instructive feedback to those you are developing. Feedback, of course, is not about being right or about making a point. The motivation of God-honoring feedback is ultimately for the good of the friend you love. People long for feedback, to know how they are doing and how they can improve. The former chief learning officer at Goldman Sachs, Steve Kerr, said, "Practice without feedback is like bowling through a curtain that hangs down at knee level."

3. Implement: Put Steel in the Ground

After you have designed the leadership pipeline, you must implement it among your leaders. Actually, you must continually implement. Your leadership pipeline will not serve you well if you roll it out one time and expect people to embrace it as a helpful construct.

Communicate clearly. Understanding always precedes commitment, and people will not be able to understand the leadership pipeline and their opportunities for development unless there is clarity. Placing the pipeline before leadership teams helps them see the overall plan to develop and deploy leaders.

Communicate carefully. The pipeline must be communicated carefully, however, because you don't want to send the signal that success is progression through the pipeline. The goal of the pipeline is development, not progression. There are some on your team who sense the Lord has called them to their craft, not to oversee others in their craft. There are some who serve faithfully in the work force, who represent Christ genuinely, who do not desire to manage and direct leaders. They are designed to influence and lead where they are, and do not envision "managing more people." Success is not moving through steps in a pipeline, but faithfully fulfilling the Lord's purpose and plan for your life. Success is not progression through the pipeline, but rather being developed for His glory.

Mark transition moments. A small group leader who moves to coaching other small group leaders must make a mental transition from shepherding people to recruiting, shepherding, and training leaders. A greeter in your church who moves into training and leading other greeters must change his or her approach. Shaking hands becomes recruiting other leaders to shake hands and ensuring people are properly scheduled. You can utilize the leadership pipeline to help people understand how they will need to lead differently if they move to greater levels of responsibility. Leaders often fail in their new roles because they default to what they were doing before instead of leading differently based on the new role.

Don't leapfrog. Both of us have led churches that have experienced seasons of exponential growth. In those seasons the need for new leaders is so pressing that there is a constant temptation to leapfrog your own pipeline, to take people who have been competent at one level of the pipeline and thrust them into a new place of ministry that is several steps ahead.

When you help people skip steps in development, no one wins. The people under the care of the new leader do not receive the care and leadership they need. The new leader is placed in a position in which the leader is unprepared. The ministry or organization, as a whole, suffers. While we often imagine that declining and crumbling organizations begin to fall apart because they have grown complacent, Jim Collins, in his book *How the Mighty Fall,* states that complacency is not the issue: "Decline begins when the growth of an organization outpaces the organization's ability to have the right people at the table."[9] Leapfrogging your own pipeline is one sure way to ensure you get the wrong people at the table.

4. Evaluate: Monitor Progress

After you have implemented a leadership pipeline, you must monitor the progress of the leaders your church is developing. The leadership pipeline is designed to have a large entryway and a narrow ending—meaning, not every person is going to progress through the pipeline. Some people are going to intentionally get stuck in the pipeline and won't progress. They sense they have progressed to the place the Lord has for them. While success is development and not progression, it should be the calling of God that prevents people from moving to the end of your pipeline and not lack of training or opportunities. Clogs and leaks can stop you from moving more leaders, leaders who want to be developed, through your pipeline.

Look for clogs. As you evaluate the pipeline, look for clogs. If people are consistently not moving from one level of leadership to another, you clearly have a problem. Perhaps people are not being invited to take a new step of leadership. Or perhaps training is lacking. Evaluate where clogs are taking place, listen to leaders, and look for reasons why more people are not progressing.

Look for leaks. If people are leaving (leaking out) the ministry before they have passed through the pipeline, there are likely unmet expectations. There is likely something they are not receiving that they thought they should be receiving, whether that is training or coaching. If a leak is consistent, evaluate the harmony between the promise made to new leaders and the training and coaching provided them.

Developing a leadership pipeline does not need to be as mysterious and overwhelming as it sounds to many leaders. Prayerfully, and in community, discuss how your ministry will develop leaders systematically. Start with the levels of leadership in your ministry, clarify the necessary competencies, and build training plans for those competencies. Then continually implement and evaluate. Remember, most of the competencies learned in a church ministry context will transfer to most other leadership situations. Along the way, work hard to make the pipeline personal for the people you serve.

Pathways: Make It Personal

A pipeline is for the whole organization; a pathway is an individual development plan, within the pipeline. A pipeline focuses on the flock; a pathway focuses on individual sheep.

"Pipeline" can sound so sterile, corporate, and cold, so make leadership development personal by helping people see their pathways. A pathway is simply a view of the pipeline that is tailored for the individual. It may be as simple as showing a person his place in the pipeline and the training plans designed for him. It may be as simple as helping a leader see how the training the church offers is designed to develop her. Give the people you serve a map, a picture of their development, and not merely a menu of all your church does.

There is a massive difference between offering people a menu and a map. Many church leaders offer the people in their churches a menu—a menu of all the programs, studies, activities, and events that the church programmatically offers. Essentially the message is: "Here is what we have; choose what you want." With this approach, churches have expanding menus as something can always be added. Churches with menus grow more and more complex and are likely to make less and less of an impact as energy and resources are divided in a plethora of directions. Churches who approach leadership development with a menu mentality merely advertise a list of things they can do "to develop themselves."

Other churches, and sadly this is the minority, offer people a map. The map reveals how the church strategically and intentionally uses all she offers to move people toward greater maturity in the faith. Churches with maps have a theology and philosophy of discipleship beneath their programs. In other words, they are not merely winging it. They are disciplined in their approach to discipleship. And they are disciplined in their approach to leadership development. They have a plan for helping develop the leaders and potential leaders the Lord has placed under their care.

Perhaps the biggest difference between churches with menus and churches with maps is in the leadership of those churches. Travel agents and servers offer menus and say, "Here are all the options. Best of luck." They don't join you on the adventure. They may never even experience the options they are putting before you. Tour guides offer maps and say, "Let's go on this journey together. We know the way. We have been on this journey before, and we are in this with you."

Our churches don't need spiritual travel agents who promote journeys they don't take. We need tour guides who set a wise direction, take the journey with the people, and live all that they are inviting the people to live. We need leaders who desire to create other leaders. If all we give people is a menu, we should stop bemoaning the fact that we are creating consumers.

Leaders often most struggle with "developing others." The pressures of today continually threaten to pull leaders away from being a "human capital developer." If you want to develop people who will develop others, they must see in you that development is absolutely essential. They must know, by watching your life, that part of leadership is creating and commissioning future leaders. A leadership pipeline helps you systemize and operationalize the conviction on a broad and sweeping level.

If you and your church are going to develop leaders broadly and consistently, you need a map, a systematic approach to leadership development. Pathways make pipelines serve to make leaders beyond just the local churches. Most Christian leaders will not primarily express their leadership within the structure of the church. Pathways translate leadership for God's people into the harvest field God has placed them in. Don't send your people on a cruise to nowhere. Develop a pipeline and show people their path within it.

CONTINUED . . .

*Apart from grace-driven effort, people do not
gravitate toward godliness, prayer, obedience to
Scripture, faith, and delight in the Lord.*
—D. A. CARSON

You won't drift *into* developing leaders, but you will easily drift *from* developing leaders. Just as we don't drift into a pursuit of holiness, we won't drift into developing and deploying leaders. For a church to create and commission leaders into all spheres of life, leaders must continually focus time, energy, and direction on leadership development in the local church.

Leadership development in the Church, in recent years, has emerged as both the felt need and the real need. It is hard to find yourself in a ministry conversation where people don't eventually bring up leadership development. Often felt needs are not real needs, so when churches start to long for and hunger for something that is really, and has always been, a need among God's people, we rejoice. By God's grace, people are sensing that churches are designed for much more than consumption; they are divinely designed to develop leaders.

While we are grateful for the conversations about leadership development, they will prove insufficient without conviction, culture, and constructs. You and your church are designed to lead; but for this calling to be realized, your conviction must be continually stirred, your culture must be continually managed, and your constructs must be continually implemented.

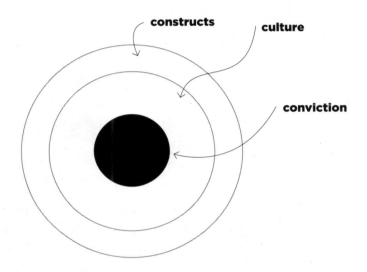

Conviction Continually Stirred

For leadership development to take root in the culture you influence, a conviction to develop others must be continually stirred in your heart. Hopefully after reading this book, your heart is stirred with the reality that the Church is the center of leadership development, and that leaders formed in your church are sent into the world to make disciples. Hopefully your passion for all of God's people serving and ministering has been fed. Hopefully you have a deeper conviction not just for developing others, but for developing others whose leadership reflects the image of God.

But this conviction will be stifled if it is not continually stirred. Life can suck the vision from a leader. There will be a myriad of things to do in developing others, because it is slow and arduous work that can easily be put aside. Expectations placed on ministry leaders, even from well-meaning people, often work against developing leaders. Sadly, people often want pastors to *do* ministry rather than equip others for it.

Yet the biggest threat to stifle conviction is the idolatry in our own hearts. Just as in other areas of our lives, our idolatry—our longing for something other than God—keeps us from obeying Him with glad hearts. A leader's idolatry will prevent a leader from the holy task of developing other leaders.

Tim Keller, David Powlison, and others have thought more deeply and written more eloquently about the idolatry that plagues our hearts. They have identified four common idols beneath the surface, idols that drive sinful and destructive behavior:

Control: a longing to have everything go according to my plan

Approval: a longing to be accepted or desired[1]

Power: a longing for influence or recognition

Comfort: a longing for pleasure

These idols will strangle the conviction for leadership development in your life. Just as Dwight L. Moody famously remarked, "Sin will keep me from the Bible, or the Bible will keep me from sin," there is a sense that Jesus-driven conviction will keep you from these idols, or these idols will keep you from developing leaders.

When the idol of control dominates a leader's heart, the leader will inevitably micromanage because after all, "no one can pull this off like I can." The result is an under-developed ministry or organization as new leaders have a difficult time being developed in an over-controlled environment. When a longing for approval reigns in a leader's heart, the leader leads to be liked rather than to fulfill the assignment faithfully. Instead of leading for the good of those the ministry or organization is designed to serve, the leader really leads so others will like him or her. When a longing for power takes root in a leader's life, selfish decision-making will be the result as the leader leads to be recognized. The motivation is not to serve and bless others but to be known. When a longing for comfort rules in a leader's heart, painful and necessary decisions are delayed. The leader fears change because comfort and routine would be disrupted.

How do you know if these idols are draining the conviction from your soul for development? What does a leader with these idols likely think or say about the responsibility to develop others? Below are the four idols with accompanying thoughts or phrases leaders have muttered.

Control

I just want to ensure this gets done the right way.
I don't trust another to do it as I can do it.

If you have thought or said either of the above, your struggle with control is hampering your development of others. A leader with control issues is a leader who fails at a chief leadership task: developing others. A leader who struggles with handing significant responsibility to others fails to provide necessary experiences that aid in development.

Approval

The people need me to be the one who does this.
If someone else does this, people will flock to that person instead of me.

If you have thought or said either of the above, your longing for approval is hurting you and the people you lead. A leader who needs affection and approval from others is reluctant to develop and deploy other leaders because the leader fears the affection and approval could be divided.

Power

If someone else does this, I won't be needed any longer.
If someone else does this, people will think I am not
doing my job.

If you have thought or said either of these, you likely love to be a leader so you can be seen as a leader. You love your title (leader) more than your task (developing others). A leader whose chief desire is to be perceived as a powerful leader will ignore the greater and more important work of developing others.

Comfort

It would take too much time from other things for me to
develop leaders.
I would have to adjust my leadership approach to include
others.

If you have said or thought either of these about developing others, your desire for comfort or the status quo is keeping you from doing the difficult, messy, and painstakingly slow work of investing in future leaders. A longing for comfort will keep a leader focused on the short-term, the temporary, and the easy. Leadership development is none of these as it takes time, has eternal ramifications, and is hard work.

The idolatry of leaders impacts more than just the leaders, as teams and entire organizations are affected. Therefore, as we develop leaders we must help recognize our own proclivity to idolatry and continually repent of it. Are any of these idols stopping you or your team from developing others? We are wise to heed the apostle John's encouragement: "Guard yourselves from idols" (1 John 5:21). If we don't continually repent, we will neglect one of our chief roles as a leader.

Your conviction for developing others will be continually stirred as you gaze at the beauty of Christ and allow Him to continually give you a love and passion for His Church. His Church in your context is a community of gifted people, not a community of people with only a gifted pastor. As that truth continually grips your heart, you will lead with deep conviction.

Culture Continually Managed

Leaders, including ministry leaders, must be continually cultivating the culture they are stewarding. If you don't manage and shape the culture, you are ignoring the environment that the people you serve alongside live in. By "culture" we are, again, referring to the actual beliefs and shared values that drive behavior. For leadership development to really work itself out in your context, then developing others must be a shared valued that drives behavior.

If a church leader attempts to implement a strategy without first addressing the culture, and the two are in conflict with one another, the strategy is doomed before it even launches. Culture will win. And while the doctrinal confession in a church is absolutely critical, if the culture is in conflict with the confession, the culture will trump the confession.

For example, FBC of Orthodoxy has the doctrinal confession that all believers are priests and ministers because Jesus' sacrificial death for us tore the veil of separation and His Spirit has empowered all believers. They wordsmith their doctrinal statement and proudly display it on their website, in their church bulletin, and in their bylaws and constitution. But FBC of Orthodoxy has a long-standing culture that the "real ministers" are the professional clergy—that whenever a need arises, it lands on a staff member's plate. When a tragedy occurs, when someone needs counseling, the first thought is which "staff pastor" should handle this. And staff love to work for FBC of Orthodoxy. The church is in a great area to raise a family, pays those "who minister" really well for the understanding that they will do the ministry. It is the culture that drives the behavior, not the doctrinal confession.

Managing culture is not something that is done just once; culture must be continually shaped. Tony Hsieh (founder and CEO of Zappos) tells the story about his former company, LinkExchange, which was sold to Microsoft for 265 million dollars. When the company was just getting started, Tony and his friends loved the culture. They worked together all the time, sometimes forgetting what day it was. As the company initially grew, they hired their friends, people who shared the same values and understood the culture of the team. But as they continued to grow, "they ran out of friends to hire." In other words, people began to join the team who did not share the same values. And the culture quickly deteriorated, so much so that Tony said he no longer wanted to come to work at his own company.

Because of that experience, he now obsesses over cultural fit at Zappos, and encourages other leaders to do the same. Over half of an employee's annual evaluation is based on living their values, and he has said, "An employee can be a superstar in job performance, but if they don't live up to core values, we will fire them just for that."[2]

Wise ministry leaders will continually check the culture and, by God's grace, seek to bring it into deep alignment with the theology and ministry philosophy of the church. How does one check culture and how can one reinforce values that you want bolstered in the culture? Here are three simple questions to ask yourself as you seek to lead the culture in your sphere of influence:

What is celebrated? Plato famously said, "Whatever is celebrated in a country is cultivated there." He was right. Whatever is celebrated in a church is cultivated there. Leaders are wise to be careful and strategic with what they celebrate. Celebrate and point to those who are living the values you want reinforced. If you celebrate the wrong things, you will get a culture you didn't desire.

By listening to the *stories* of celebration, you can determine what has been cultivated through the years. By understanding who are held up as *heroes* in a culture, you can discern what is really valued. Both heroes and stories reveal what is deeply important. Who the group holds up as the heroes to emulate and what is celebrated as "a win" gives a clear snapshot of culture. Listen for the heroes and the stories to learn a culture, and if you want to shape culture, utilize heroes and stories.

Heroes and stories are powerful in building ministry culture. In a church, the ultimate Hero must be Jesus. He alone can bear the responsibility for His people. If you want to build a culture of "leadership development," point continually to our *Hero*, who has made us all priests by His sacrifice for us. And constantly tell *stories* of people who are being developed and deployed. Celebrate when groups disciple others well. Manage culture with celebration.

What is prayed for? As you sit in meetings and other gatherings, listen to the prayers. You can learn a lot about the culture of a church by listening to the prayers of the leaders within the church. For example, a church that is externally focused prays for those who are not yet His. A church that desires to bless and serve the community prays for the city where the church is located. A church that values leaders being developed prays for new leaders, and new leaders pray for the opportunities the Lord has given them to represent Christ in the world. You can see what is really important in the culture of a church by listening to the prayers.

In the same way, you can help people long to represent Christ in their spheres of influence by thanking the Lord for sovereignly putting the people in the church where they are and pleading with Him to use His people as salt and light. As Jesus saw people harassed and helpless, He declared how plentiful the harvest will be in His Kingdom and commanded the disciples to pray for the Lord to send workers into His harvest. May we do the same in our churches. May we recognize the hurting people in our communities and ask the Lord to develop people in our churches who will be deployed to the harvest.

What is funded? Because culture is formed by the shared values tightly held by a group of people, it is helpful to distinguish between *actual* values and *aspirational* values. *Actual* values are values that are actually in the culture and clearly seen by newcomers because they are lived out. They are pronounced via people more than they are pronounced via paper. *Aspirational* values are values that leaders want a church to have but are not yet in the culture. They are often on paper but not in the hearts of the people.[3]

One way to determine if a value is *actual* or aspirational is to look at the budget. We fund whatever we value the most. You can learn a lot about what a church culture values by looking at the budget. If you want to move "developing others" from an aspirational value to an actual value, budget decisions will need to be made. Financing the development of people will look different from context to context, but if development is important then finances will flow that direction.

Constructs Continually Implemented

Some have equated organizational culture with personality. In the 1920s, Alfred Adler proposed that for a person to have a healthy and strong personality, there must be harmony between how the person sees himself and how others perceive him. We have all seen folks who think they are kind and compassionate, yet everyone else thinks they are jerks. These are clearly unhealthy people with a warped view of reality. Organizations are the same way. In a healthy context, there is alignment between what is said to be valued and believed and what actually is.[4]

Constructs help reinforce the culture of leadership development because they continually show people that developing and deploying leaders is "essential around here." Implementing a leadership pipeline and developing leaders is not something that is easy, and it is not something that can be done only once. Continual implementation is a must.

Many churches never realize the full potential of their plans or strategies because they switch them too frequently. They abandon their direction for a new direction and confuse the people as to where the church is really headed. Implementing and abandoning or neglecting a leadership pipeline will perhaps do more harm than good because the lack of discipline will lower the credibility of the leadership.

You must stick with it even when few seem to understand. It always takes significantly longer than most leaders realize for a major initiative to gain traction, much more so a major initiative that is so counterintuitive to many of the people in the church. If leadership development has not been a priority, rolling out a leadership pipeline one weekend will not suddenly make it such. It will take continual implementation in the same direction.

A Case Study of Austin Stone

After taking a church planting class in seminary, Matt Carter moved from The Woodlands, Texas, to plant The Austin Stone Community Church. The most compelling reason for this daring move from the fast-growing Houston area was simple: Austin needed the gospel. In the early 2000s, Austin, Texas, was (and still is) an anomaly in the South. Right in the middle of the Bible Belt sits a progressive, fast-growing, but significantly unreached city called Austin, Texas. It's weird. And it aims to be!

A couple years later, I (Kevin) joined the team of this remarkably fast-growing church. Having grown up a non-Christian in Austin, the opportunity to jump in with a church making much of Jesus was something I just couldn't miss.

By 2004 The Austin Stone had already grown to several hundreds of people in worship. One major caveat: nearly all were college students or young professionals. Don't get me wrong; we believed this to be an incredible blessing. But still, there were several tricky, looming problems that had to be solved. As our church grew, we needed leaders. We didn't just need helpers and volunteers; we needed leaders with significant capacity. We lacked resources inside the church.

As a church plant in a relatively unchurched area, we didn't pick up any "free agent" Christian sages to fill the leadership need. Making things more difficult, we couldn't even go out and hire one. As you might expect, the giving was quite light in a church with an average age of about twenty-three. Many of our friends and contemporaries leading young churches were providentially located next to great seminaries with a seemingly endless supply of men and women already dedicated to serving God and growing in Christian leadership. Even better, these students created for local churches a supply and demand relationship for opportunities to serve that minimized the need to pay many of them. *Hey, if you get the chance to pick up good leaders who need a place to lead, are being trained by great Christian institutions, and don't expect much money—take it!* Providentially, this wasn't an option for Austin Stone.

Our situation was a gift. We, like so many others, knew it was our job to equip the saints for ministry, but our environment encouraged us to go "all in" on this *conviction*.

We started fostering the *culture* of leadership development throughout the ministry by bringing light to God's design for development and telling stories of everyday people being equipped to do extraordinary things. The application of this conviction started small. The first stab at this was taking nine men into my (Kevin's) home to focus on growth in character, doctrine, and skill. Over the years, these men have become, by God's grace, incredibly influential leaders. These men are leading their families, businesses, and churches. Over the years, the aim is the same but we have built out the structure to allow more leaders to be developed.

The *constructs* have been critical. The Austin Stone Institute was created in 2011 with the expressed desire to create godly leaders for church and for the world. Every year more than three hundred future leaders enter the program. This program, as a part of the development ecosystem at The Stone, involves a robust application process, coaching structures for each student, character, doctrine and skill curricula, written and oral assessments, practical ministry experience, and placement structures. The institute offers pathways for several different leadership roles so that the church may produce leaders for various domains in society.

The Austin Stone has embraced the calling of leadership development well beyond the need to simply fill our own internal volunteer needs. Instead, the church is joining God's desire to use the church to fill the earth with the kind of leaders God has designed to lead. One of the most often noted expressions of this commitment is found in our development of worship leaders through the institute. So many churches throughout the world are in need of great worship leaders, and The Austin Stone is no different. Yet, in order to honor the commitment to train and send great leaders into the world, The Austin Stone not only trains great leaders but posts their profiles, résumés, and work on a website so that others can offer them positions to serve and lead. Sure, we would love to keep our best, but a construct for leadership development that honors God's design for the local church must include deployment. This deployment must have the world in scope. Without deployment platforms outside the church, the church isn't developing leaders for God's global purpose.

These God-honoring development constructs cost much more than losing a few great leaders inside the church. Every three years, The Austin Stone aims to send more than one hundred missionaries long-term, to unreached peoples. Not only are these leaders of great capacity, but also the quantity being sent creates strain on the church. Nonetheless, God is the One who sends.

The systems and structures of our church must be built to send every single leader God is calling to the world. In many cases, we must ask ourselves if our constructs are barriers to God's call on future leaders. In the case of The Austin Stone, as we have built the constructs, we have been utterly shocked at how many leaders God has called from our church into His mission. If the Church of Jesus Christ is to be an epicenter of leadership development, then we must be ready and willing to send quality and quantity into His harvest.

Please Continue

Your church is unique. The passion of the leaders, the local context, and the gifting of those the Lord has put in your church all combine to make your church different from every other church. Yes, God wants to do something very specific in your context, but at the same time there are some things that are nonnegotiable for every church that gathers in the name of Jesus and is centered on His work for us. In other words, developing leaders must not be seen as optional for our churches, for your church.

In our individualized culture, church leaders often want an identity that is highly unique, one that is "just for us," one that shows "no one else is quite like us." But we must be careful. The foundation of our faith is something we have received. It is not something that we develop, create, or improve. It is "the faith that was delivered to the saints once for all" (Jude 3). It must not be unique. Nor should our commitment to disciple people and develop leaders. Though expressed differently from context to context, God's people must be deeply committed to developing and deploying leaders.

The Christian faith has continued to advance because the Lord has continually raised up new leaders to disciple others. The Kingdom of God has continually advanced because God's people have been developed and deployed to make disciples. The spreading of the faith is going to continue until people from every tribe, tongue, and nation are His. By His grace, He has invited us to join Him.

For the faith to continually advance in your context, your conviction must be continually stirred, your culture continually cultivated, and your constructs continually implemented.

Please continue . . .

APPENDIX

JESUS AND DISCIPLESHIP: SELECTIONS FROM THE GOSPELS

KNOWLEDGE — EXPERIENCES — COACHING

When daylight came, He summoned His disciples, and He chose 12 of them—He also named them apostles.
—LUKE 6:13

Knowledge (*The disciples* heard)

Moments where Jesus taught His disciples or they heard Jesus teaching a crowd:

- After calling His disciples, Jesus immediately ministered to and taught crowds. In Jesus' sermon, His disciples learned the values of the Kingdom, the offense of hypocrisy, and the importance of building one's life on the solid foundation (Luke 6:17–49, cf. Matt. 5–7).
- The disciples heard Jesus' affirmation of John the Baptist and learned that humility and obedience are essential values in God's Kingdom (Luke 7:24–30).
- After teaching the parable of the soils to the crowd, Jesus shared the meaning with His disciples (Luke 8:4–15).

- Jesus disclosed His identity and upcoming death and resurrection to His disciples (Luke 9:18–21).
- Both in hearing His teaching to the crowd and His responses to people claiming they wanted to follow Him, the disciples learned the cost of following Jesus (Luke 9:23–26, 57–62).
- Jesus privately shared with His disciples how they were blessed to see what they were seeing (Luke 10:23–24).
- Even as a massive crowd gathered, Jesus spoke "first to His disciples" about the hypocrisy of the Pharisees, fearing God, and their value to Him (Luke 12:1–7).
- After someone asked questions about an inheritance, Jesus spoke to His disciples about not worrying, trusting God, seeking Him first, and being prepared (Luke 12:13–40). Peter was not sure if the message was just for the disciples or for everyone (as in, "Jesus, You are teaching *all* this to us in front of everyone?"). Jesus continued speaking to His disciples about faithfulness and suffering (Luke 12:41–53).
- The disciples heard Jesus teach through many parables to the religious and in response to the religious (Luke 14–16).
- Jesus told the parable of the shrewd manager to His disciples, challenging them to be astute with the Kingdom of God (Luke 16:1–13).
- When asked about the coming Kingdom, Jesus gave the religious a brief answer and spent significantly more time speaking to His disciples (Luke 17:20–37).
- Jesus shared the parable of the persistent widow with the Twelve, encouraging them to be persistent in prayer (Luke 18:1–8).
- The disciples heard the parable of the sinner and the tax collector, and Jesus' emphasis on a sinner being justified only by mercy (Luke 18:9–14).

- Jesus denounced the religious in front of His disciples, teaching them about the futility and danger of cleansing the outside of the cup (Matt. 23).
- John devoted four chapters to Jesus' Farewell Discourse (John 14–17), where Jesus instructed His disciples and prayed for them. He gave them knowledge about the Holy Spirit, encouraged them to love one another, assured them of persecution and peace, and challenged them to stay connected to the Vine and bear fruit.

Experiences *(The disciples* observed *or* participated)

Moments where Jesus taught the disciples by living in front of them or by serving alongside them:

- The disciples watched Jesus' zeal for prayer and for the Father's house (John 2:17).
- The disciples found Jesus praying and learned His dependence on the Father (Mark 1:35–37).
- Jesus handed responsibilities to His disciples, including baptizing people (John 4:2).
- The disciples were amazed that Jesus was talking to a woman, as He was showing them that His grace transcends cultural boundaries (John 4:27).
- The disciples saw Jesus affirm the faith of the men who "unroofed" Peter's roof to bring a paralyzed man to Jesus, observing that people are much more important than possessions, even better than roofs, *even Peter's roof* (Mark 2:1–12).
- The disciples watched Jesus spend time with tax collectors and be accused of "being a friend of sinners"—certainly impacting their pursuit of people far from God (Matt. 9:9–13).

- Jesus invited Peter to walk on water with Him, to experience a miracle alongside Him (John 6:16–21; Matt. 14:22–33).
- The disciples watched as Jesus cried alongside Mary and Martha, certainly impacting how they would later help others in moments of pain (John 11:35).
- The disciples watched as Jesus healed a centurion's servant and praised his faith, learning the gospel would be for those outside the Jewish heritage (Luke 7:1–10).
- Jesus went to Peter's house to minister to his mother-in-law (Matt. 8:14–17).
- From watching Jesus' interaction with the sinful woman, the disciples learned how to show mercy to those the religious viewed as shameful (Luke 7:36–50).
- Jesus invited Peter, James, and John into where Jairus's daughter lay dead, before Jesus raised her. They watched Him minister in the midst of grief (Luke 8:51–53).
- When Jesus fed the five thousand, He involved His disciples in the miracle. He asked them to get food, knowing they could not. And the disciples passed out the baskets and collected the leftovers (Luke 9:12–17).
- Jesus picked grain with His disciples on the Sabbath, and He engaged the religious leaders on the purpose of the Sabbath as they watched (Matt. 12:1–8).
- When Jesus fed the four thousand, He involved the disciples in the feeding and serving of the people. They experienced the miracle with Him (Matt. 15:32–39).
- Jesus took Peter, James, and John up on the mountain to pray, where they saw the Transfiguration of Christ (Luke 9:28–36).
- The disciples learned from watching Jesus' affirmation of Mary that intimacy with God is more valuable than service to Him (Luke 10:38–42).

- As Jesus showed the foolishness of the argument that His power was from Satan, the disciples learned how to respond to critics and those seeking to "test Him" (Luke 11:15–28).
- The disciples watched how Jesus answered questions on current events and turned them into opportunities to call people to repentance (Luke 13:1–9).
- In Jericho, the disciples observed ministry to the poor (a blind man begging) and ministry to the rich (Zacchaeus). They watched as Jesus pursued and loved people from different backgrounds (Luke 18:35—19:9).
- Jesus involved the disciples in the triumphal entry by sending two of His disciples to get the donkey that He would ride (Luke 19:28–31).
- Jesus used a visit to the temple to jump-start a discussion with His disciples about the future (Matt. 24:1–2).
- Jesus involved His disciples in preparation for the Passover by sending Peter and John to prepare (Luke 22:7–13).
- The night in the Upper Room (Luke 22; John 13) provided the disciples with an experience they would never forget, as God washed their feet.
- In the agony of the Garden of Gethsemane, Jesus showed His disciples how to trust God in the midst of pain (Matt. 26:36).

Coaching (The disciples had truth applied)

Moments where Jesus taught His disciples by responding to a situation or question or by asking them questions:

- When people began to stop following Jesus, He asked the Twelve if they were going to leave too (John 6:66–70).
- When Jesus ministered to the crowds with His disciples, they saw His compassion and He used the moment to

challenge them to pray for workers in the harvest (Matt. 9:35–38).

- The disciples attempted a theological debate over a blind man ("who sinned, this man or his parents?"), and Jesus responded, "This came about so that God's works might be displayed in him" (John 9:1–3).
- Jesus used Judas's question about "wasteful worship" to emphasize that He would only be with His disciples a short period of time (John 12:4–8).
- After calming the storm, Jesus asks a penetrating question: "Where is your faith?" (Luke 8:22–25).
- Jesus sent the Twelve out to minister to those who were hurting. When they returned, they shared their experiences with Him. Essentially, they debriefed (Luke 9:1–10).
- After the disciples could not cast a demon out, Jesus challenged the disciples on their faith and emphasized that "this kind does not come out except by prayer and fasting" (Luke 9:37–42; cf. Matt. 17:21).
- When Jesus perceived that they were arguing about who was the greatest, Jesus confronted the disciples with an object lesson on humility—a child (Luke 9:46–48).
- When the disciples were concerned about others using the name of Jesus, Jesus taught the disciples how to respond to others in ministry (Luke 9:49–50).
- When James and John wanted to destroy people with fire, Jesus confronted them for their lack of love (Luke 9:51–56).
- Jesus sent more disciples, not only the Twelve, to serve and preach. When they returned excited about the fruit of their ministry, Jesus challenged them to rejoice that their names are written in heaven (Luke 10:1–20).
- Peter approached Jesus with questions about the parable about what defiles a man, and Jesus explained in greater detail to His disciples (Matt. 15:15–20).

- When hearing the disciples express concern over forgetting bread, Jesus challenged them in their lack of faith (Matt. 16:1–12).
- After Peter was asked about Jesus paying taxes, Jesus utilized the moment to teach about liberty and responsibility in our culture (Matt. 17:24–27).
- The teaching Jesus offered His disciples about forgiving others was in response to Peter's question about the depth of forgiveness (Matt. 18:21–35).
- After James and John's mom embarrassingly asks for the best seats for her sons, Jesus uses the moment to confront them on their selfishness and remind them that His Kingdom consists of humility and suffering, as He ultimately came here to serve us (Mark 10:35–45).
- Jesus cursed a fig tree and used the moment to teach His disciples about faith (Matt. 21:18–22).
- After watching Jesus continually pray, the disciples asked Jesus to teach them. Jesus gave them an example of how to pray and challenged them to be persistent in prayer (Luke 11:1–12).
- When the disciples asked Jesus to increase their faith, Jesus challenged them to expect no special rewards for basic obedience (Luke 17:1–10).
- Jesus corrected His disciples for stopping children from coming to Him, and used the moment to remind them of childlike faith (Luke 18:15–16).
- After the rich young ruler walked away sad, the disciples were astonished. Jesus encouraged them that all they left to follow Him was not in vain (Luke 18:18–29; cf. Mark 10:17–31).
- Over breakfast, after His resurrection, Jesus restored Peter (John 21).

NOTES

Introduction

1. We use Church (capital C) when referring to the universal body of Christ and church (lowercase c) when referring to a local church.

2. See http://www.gty.org/blog/B130207/what-does-it-mean -to-make-disciples.

3. There is a Proto-Indo-European word *leit* or *leith* that means "to leave, to die." "Proto-Indo-European" is a linguistic reconstruction, created by scholars, of language spoken centuries ago by those living in Europe and Asia.

4. Robert E. Quinn, *Change the World: How Ordinary People Can Accomplish Extraordinary Results* (San Francisco, CA: Jossey Bass, 2000), 179.

5. The accounts of Buddha's last words vary a bit but carry the same basic jist. For example, PBS.org indicates Buddha's dying words to be, "Strive on, untiringly." The Buddhist Education and Information Network claims his dying words were, "Work hard to gain your own salvation." Both accounts are the opposite of Jesus' dying words: "It is finished." See http://www.pbs.org /thebuddha/death-and-legacy-part-2/. See also http://www.buddha net.net/e-learning/buddhism/lifebuddha/2_322bud.htm.

Chapter 1

1. Michael Goheen, *A Light to the Nations* (Grand Rapids, MI: Baker, 2011), 115.

2. Jim Collins at http://www.jimcollins.com/article_topics /articles/aligning-action.html.

3. J. Oswald Sanders, *Spiritual Leadership* (Chicago, IL: Moody Bible Institute, 2004), 79.

4. The book *Return on Character*, by Fred Kiel, is referenced in *Harvard Business Review*, April 2015. Kiel discovered in his research that companies led by leaders of character outperformed their counterparts. Kiel defines character as integrity, responsibility, compassion, and forgiveness.

5. "Measuring the Return on Character" *Harvard Business Review* (April 2015), https://hbr.org/2015/04/measuring-the-return-on-character.

6. James M. Kouzes and Barry Z. Posner, *The Leadership Challenge* (San Francisco, CA: Jossey-Bass, 2007), 36. This research-based book shows, in part, that what organizations and people want most in their leaders is credibility.

7. In his helpful book, *The New Reformation*, Greg Ogden credits John Stott with the term omni-competent and emphasizes that the body of Christ "is a gifted people not a gifted pastor."

Chapter 2

1. In a 2012 LifeWay Research project, more than one thousand pastors were asked about their churches' plans for leadership development and equipping the people in their church for ministry. Only 25 percent of all leaders surveyed could express any type of plan.

2. See www.youhadonejob.org.

3. John Piper articulates in this post that pastors/elders have two chief responsibilities: teaching and leading. We agree with his view of the office of pastor and are simply suggesting that the goal of both is the quipping of God's people: See http://www .desiringgod.org/resource/elders-pastors-bishops-and-bethlehem.

4. Edmund Clowney, *Called to the Ministry* (Phillipsburg, NJ: P&R Publishing, 1976), 41.

5. Elton Trueblood, *The Incendiary Fellowship* (New York, NY: Harper and Row, 1967), 41.

6. John Stott, *The Message of Ephesians: The Bible Speaks Today* series (Leicester, UK: InterVarsity Press, 1979), 167.

7. Philip Graham Ryken and Michael LeFebvre, *Our Triune God: Living in the Love of the Three-in-One* (Wheaton, IL: Crossway, 2011), 105.

8. See http://www.sjsu.edu/people/andrew.fleck/courses/Hum1b Spr15/Lecture_25%20Luther_Lotzer_Calvin.pdf.

Chapter 3

1. "The Best-Performing CEOs in the World," *Harvard Business Review*, November 2014.

2. See http://www.nytimes.com/2015/08/16/technology/inside -amazon-wrestling-big-ideas-in-a-bruising-workplace.html.

3. See http://www.nytimes.com/2015/08/19/technology/amazon -workplace-reactions-comments.html.

4. Peter J. Gentry and Stephen J. Wellum, *God's Kingdom through God's Covenants: A Concise Biblical Theology* (Wheaton, IL: Crossway, 2015), Kindle edition.

5. See http://www.npr.org/sections/thetwo-way/2015/08/17/ 432555175/jeff-bezos-responds-to-new-york-times-report-on-amazons-workplace.

Chapter 4

1. George Eldon Ladd, *The Gospel of the Kingdom: Scriptural Studies in the Kingdom of God* (Grand Rapids, MI; Cambridge, UK: Eerdmans, 1959), 21.

2. J. I. Packer, *Concise Theology: A Guide to Historic Christian Beliefs* (Wheaton, IL: Tyndale, 1993).

3. Eryn Sun, "John Stott: 10 Memorable Quotes," *Christian Post* (July 28, 2011), http://www.christianpost.com/news/10-beloved-quotes-by-reverend-john-stott-53021/.

4. Wayne Grudem, *Business for the Glory of God: The Bible's Teaching on the Moral Goodness of Business* (Wheaton, IL: Good News Publishers, 2003), Kindle Locations 254–58.

5. Sebastian Traeger and Greg D. Gilbert, *The Gospel at Work: How Working for King Jesus Gives Purpose and Meaning to Our Jobs* (Grand Rapids, MI: Zondervan, 2013), 66.

6. Stuart Ewen and Elizabeth Ewen, *Channels of Desire: Mass Images and the Shaping of American Consciousness* (Minneapolis, MN: University of Minnesota Press, 1992), 24.

7. Timothy Keller, *Gospel Contextualization: Center Church: Part Three* (Grand Rapids, MI: Zondervan, 2013), Kindle edition.

8. R. J. Krejcir, Francis A. Schaeffer Institute of Church Leadership Development, http://www.truespirituality.org. Retrieved 07/10/2015 from http://www.intothyword.org/apps/articles/default.asp?articleid=36562&columnid=3958.

9. J. Oswald Sanders, *Spiritual Leadership: A Commitment to Excellence for Every Believer* (Chicago, IL: Moody Publishers, 2007), Kindle Locations 188–90.

10. Timothy S. Laniak, *Shepherds After My Own Heart* (Downers Grove, IL: InterVarsity, 2006), 247.

Chapter 5

1. Kevin Peck, "Examing a Church Culture of Multiplication: A Multiple Case Study," http://digital.library.sbts.edu/handle/10392/4621.

2. Philip Towner, *The Goal of Our Instruction: The Structure of Theology and Ethics in the Pastoral Epistles* (London, UK: Bloomsbury Academic, 2015), 133.

3. John Piper and David Mathis, *Finish the Mission: Bringing the Gospel to the Unreached and Unengaged* (Wheaton, IL: Crossway, 2012), 114.

4. Robert Duncan Culver, *Systematic Theology: Biblical and Historical* (Ross-shire, UK: Mentor, 2005), 44.

5. Carl Friedrich Keil and Franz Delitzsch, *Commentary on the Old Testament*, vol. 5 (Peabody, MA: Hendrickson, 1996), 295.

6. J. R. Watson, ed., *An Annotated Anthology of Hymns* (Oxford: Oxford University Press, 2002), 216.

7. According to Edgar Schein, "The most common manifestation of this belief system seen in the world of organizational culture is in the office." Concerning the office, Schein notices, "One of the most obvious ways that rank and status are symbolized in organizations is by the location and size of offices." The local church will manifest its perspective on space most obviously in the locations of worship, and to a lesser degree the church office (Schein, *Organizational Culture*, 135).

8. George R. Beasley-Murray, *John,* Word Biblical Commentary, vol. 36 (Dallas, TX: Word, 2002), 61.

9. John Peter Lange, et al., *A Commentary on the Holy Scriptures: Acts* (Bellingham, WA: Logos Bible Software, 2008), 13–14.

10. L. Berkhof, *Systematic Theology* (Grand Rapids, MI: Eerdmans, 1938), 209.

11. Ibid.

12. Norman Geisler, *Systematic Theology,* vol. 3 (Minneapolis, MN: Bethany, 2004), 125.

13. Douglas J. Moo, *The Epistle to the Romans,* The New International Commentary on the New Testament (Grand Rapids, MI: Eerdmans, 1996), 201.

14. See http://www.lifeway.com/pastors/2015/07/29/the-state-of-american-theology.

15. Culver, *Systematic Theology,* 256.

16. In Acts 15:39 Paul refuses to work with John Mark after a ministry failure related to fear. Barnabas continues to work with the young leader. Later, in 2 Timothy 4:11, Paul asks Timothy to bring the same John Mark and refers to him as useful.

17. James D. G. Dunn, *Romans 1–8,* Word Biblical Commentary, vol. 38A (Dallas, TX: Word, 1998), 463.

18. According to Romans 8:16–17, "The Spirit Himself testifies with our spirit that we are God's children, and if children, also heirs—heirs of God and coheirs with Christ—seeing that we suffer with Him so that we may also be glorified with Him."

19. Gordon D. Fee, *The First Epistle to the Corinthians,* The New International Commentary on the New Testament (Grand Rapids, MI: Eerdmans, 1987), 602.

20. Berkhof, *Systematic Theology,* 450.

21. F. F. Bruce, *The Epistles to the Colossians, to Philemon, and to the Ephesians,* The New International Commentary on the New Testament (Grand Rapids, MI: Eerdmans, 1984), 353.

22. Bruce J. Avolio, *Full Range Leadership Development,* 2nd ed. (Thousand Oaks, CA: SAGE Publications, 2010), 8.

23. Ibid., (Kindle Locations 3238–40).

24. Stephen S. Smalley, *1, 2, 3 John,* Word Biblical Commentary, vol. 51 (Dallas, TX: Word, 1989), 239.

25. Norman L. Geisler, *Systematic Theology*, vol. 4: *Church, Last Things* (Minneapolis, MN: Bethany House Publishers, 2005), 49.

26. Edwin A. Blum, *1 Peter*, ed. Frank E. Gaebelein, *The Expositor's Bible Commentary*, Vol. 12: *Hebrews Through Revelation* (Grand Rapids, MI: Zondervan, 1981), 230.

27. Andrew T. Lincoln, *Ephesians*, Word Biblical Commentary, vol. 42 (Dallas, TX: Word, 1990), 61.

28. Paul writes in Ephesians 1:20–23, "He demonstrated this power in the Messiah by raising Him from the dead and seating Him at His right hand in the heavens—far above every ruler and authority, power and dominion, and every title given, not only in this age but also in the one to come. And He put everything under His feet and appointed Him as head over everything for the church, which is His body, the fullness of the One who fills all things in every way."

29. Geisler, *Systematic Theology*, vol. 4, 67.

30. Ibid., 109.

31. Jonathan Leeman and Michael Horton, *Church Membership: How the World Knows Who Represents Jesus*, 1st ed. (Wheaton, IL: Crossway, 2012), 30.

32. Peter H. Davids, *The First Epistle of Peter*, The New International Commentary on the New Testament (Grand Rapids, MI: Eerdmans, 1990), 181.

33. Clinton William Lowin, *An Assessment of the Missional Model of Graduate Theological Education: A Case Study*, PhD Dissertation at The Southern Baptist Theological Seminary, 2009, 25.

Chapter 6

1. J. R. Woodward and Alan Hirsch, *Creating a Missional Culture: Equipping the Church for the Sake of the World* (Downers Grove, IL: InterVarsity, 2012), 30–31.

2. Edgar H. Schein, *Organizational Culture and Leadership*, 4th ed. (San Francisco, CA: Jossey-Bass, 2010), 24.

3. Jim Collins, *Built to Last: Successful Habits of Visionary Companies* (New York, NY: HarperCollins, 1994), 122.

4. For more on this, read *For the City: Proclaiming and Living Out the Gospel*, by Matt Carter and Darin Patrick.

5. Jeff Suderman, "Using the Organizational Cultural Assessment (OCAI) as a Tool for New Team Development," *Journal of Practical Consulting* 4. no. 1 (Fall/Winter 2012): 52–58.

6. See Alan Deutschman, *Change or Die* (New York, NY: HarperCollins, 2007).

7. William Bridges, *Managing Transitions: Making the Most of Change* (Philadelphia, PA: Da Capo Press, 2009), 130.

8. Suderman, "Using the Organizational Cultural Assessment," 53.

9. Joey Cochran, "Leading the Church through Grief of Sin," *9Marks*. Accessed July 14, 2015, http://9marks.org/article/leading-the-church-through-grief-of-sin.

10. Tony Merida, *Faithful Preaching* (Nashville, TN: B&H Publishing Group, 2009), 196.

11. Kim S. Cameron and Robert E. Quinn, *Diagnosing and Changing Organizational Culture: Based on the Competing Values Framework*, 3rd ed. (San Francisco, CA: Jossey-Bass, 2011), 13.

Constructs Part

1. Robert Sutton and Huggy Rao, *Scaling Up Excellence* (Crown Business, 2014).

Chapter 7

1. Robert Coleman, *The Master Plan of Evangelism* (Grand Rapids, MI: Revell, 1993), 21.

2. For a historical view of how the Church moved to an unbiblical model of ministry, the work of Alexandre Faivre is helpful.

3. Alister McGrath, "The State of the Church Before the Reformation," *Modern Reformation* 3:2 (March/April 1994): 4–11.

4. Michael Horton, "The Meaning of Ministry in the Reformed Tradition," http://www.monergism.com/thethreshold/articles/onsite/whataboutbob.html.

5. Daniel Goleman, *Primal Leadership: Unleashing the Power of Emotional Intelligence* (Boston, MA: Harvard Business School Press, 2013).

6. Charles H. Spurgeon, *Come Ye Children* (Scotland, UK: Christian Focus, 1994 repr.), 27–28.

7. Eric Geiger, Michael Kelley, and Philip Nation, *Transformational Discipleship* (Nashville, TN: B&H Publishing Group, 2012).

8. William R. Yount, *Teaching Ministry of the Church*, 2nd ed. (Nashville, TN: B&H Publishing Group, 2008).

9. Ram Charan, *Leaders at All Levels* (San Francisco, CA: Jossey-Bass, 2008), 12.

10. Noel M. Tichey, *The Leadership Engine* (New York, NY: HarperBusiness, 2002), 4.

11. Michael Card, *Parable of Joy: Reflections on the Wisdom of the Book of John* (Nashville, TN: Thomas Nelson, 1995).

12. Other authors on discipleship have noted the process Jesus used to move His disciples progressively to greater maturity and responsibility. Bill Hull, in *Jesus Christ, Disciplemaker*, notes three phases of Jesus' discipleship:
  - Come and See
  - Come and Follow Me
  - Come and Be with Me

Bill Hull, *Jesus Christ, Disciplemaker* (Grand Rapids, MI: Baker, 1984, 2004), 175.

13. Educators, such as Benjamin Bloom (Bloom's Taxonomy of Learning), have emphasized the importance of teaching that targets all domains. The cognitive domain is the mind (head). The affective domain is the will (the heart). And the psychomotor domain is the hands.

14. The zeal and knowledge example comes from Blaise Pascal, who wrote in his *Pensées*: "Four kinds of persons: zeal without knowledge; knowledge without zeal; neither knowledge nor zeal; both zeal and knowledge. The first three condemned him. The last acquitted him, were excommunicated by the Church, and yet saved the Church." Pascal points out that the only people who followed Christ and who were subsequently persecuted for Him were those with both zeal *and* knowledge.

15. Geoff Colvin, *Talent Is Overrated: What Really Separates World-Class Performers from Everybody Else* (New York, NY: Penguin, 2008), 66.

Chapter 8

1. *The Leadership Code: Five Rules to Lead By* is a book based on a leadership framework developed via qualitative research with

consultation from leaders around the world. The authors—Dave Ulrich, Norm Smallwood, and Kate Sweetman—sought to discover the DNA of leadership by asking two basic questions: (1) What percentage of effective leadership is basically the same regardless of industry, role, culture, situation, etc.? (2) Of that amount (the percentage of leadership that is the same), is there a set of common rules that leaders must master? They concluded that 60 to 70 percent of leadership is the same. And within that percentage, they identified five traits: strategist, executioner, talent manager, human capital developer, and someone who is personally proficient. According to the authors' research and observations, all great leaders have personal proficiency. Every leader has at least one other "towering strength"—one characteristic the leader excels at. However, "the higher the leader rises, the more he or she needs to develop excellence in more domains" (p. 19). And all leaders must be at least average in all domains.

2. Max DePree, "What Is Leadership" in *The Jossey-Bass Reader on Nonprofit and Public Leadership* (San Francisco, CA: Jossey-Bass, 2010), 6.

3. We reference multiple research studies that became the foundations for books. In each of the studies, one alarming and consistent thread is the lack of intentionality and focus on discipling and developing people. The studies/books we reference are: Thom S. Rainer and Eric Geiger, *Simple Church* (Nashville: B&H Publishing Group, 2006), and Ed Stetzer and Eric Geiger, *Transformational Groups* (Nashville, TN: B&H Publishing Group, 2014).

4. Atul Gawande, *The Checklist Manifesto: How to Get Things Right* (New York, NY: Metropolitan Books, 2009), 80.

5. Ibid.

6. Andy Stanley, in a Catalyst message, gave a challenging and helpful talk on systems. One of his main points is that "Systems create behaviors." We would modify his statement a little and say, "Systems *help* create behaviors." And systems help create culture. While we don't agree that systems trump content and preaching, we do agree that systems are essential, and we are grateful for Stanley's wisdom. See http://www.christianitytoday.com/le/2009/december-online-only/systemfailure.html.

7. Ram Charan, Stephen Drotter, and James Noel, *The Leadership Pipeline* (San Francisco, CA: Jossey-Bass, 2001).

8. Dave Ferguson has written and spoken about leadership pipeline. In his book, *Exponential*, he offers a helpful pipeline example. He offers their pipeline here on his blog: http://daveferguson.typepad.com/daveferguson/2007/06/leadership-less.html.

9. Jim Collins, *How the Mighty Fall: And Why Some Companies Never Give In* (New York, NY: Random House Business, 2009).

Chapter 9

1. Martin Luther said, "Under every behavioral sin is the sin of idolatry." Austin Stone, where Kevin serves as lead pastor, utilizes the helpful framework of *four root idols* to constantly call leaders and leaders being developed to repentance. The four root idols that drive our behavior are power, control, comfort, and approval. Tim Keller, David Powlinson, and Dick Keyes have written and spoken much more extensively and eloquently on the idols beneath the surface.

2. In his book *Delivering Happiness* and in multiple articles and presentations, Tony Hsieh of Zappos has spoken strongly about culture. The quote is from a presentation found at https://vimeo.com/38855860.

3. Auxano, a consulting firm for ministries, used the language "actual" values and "aspirational" values to help leaders discern the culture of their ministries. An actual value is already in the culture, and an aspirational one is one leaders must work to drive into the culture. However, it is unwise to attempt to form culture on aspirational values alone. Leaders must understand and affirm the affirmable actual values that are in the culture.

4. Jesper Kunde, *Corporate Religion* (New York, NY: Prentice Hall, 2002), 200.